Six
Psychological
Studies

Six Psychological Studies

JEAN PIAGET

With an Introduction, Notes and Glossary by
DAVID ELKIND

Translation from the French by
Anita Tenzer

Translation edited by
David Elkind

Vintage Books / A Division of Random House
NEW YORK

BP45

Editor's Introduction

꽃 ALTHOUGH JEAN PIAGET could legitimately lay claim to being a psychologist, logician, biologist, and philosopher, he is perhaps best understood as a genetic epistemologist. Like Freud, Piaget has created a new discipline which, while closely aligned with psychology, nonetheless goes beyond it in its implications for and interactions with other scientific disciplines. Genetic epistemology is essentially an experimental philosophy which seeks to answer epistemological questions through the developmental study of the child. Like any new discipline, genetic epistemology presupposes its own unique problems, method, and theory. The problems are to discover the psychological structures that underlie the formation of concepts fundamental to science. Piaget's method is the semiclinical interview—a form of nondirective inquiry centered about a verbal or practical issue. Finally, Piaget's theory, in the most general sense, is that of subject-object equilibration, the view that mental growth is governed by a continual activity aimed at balancing the intrusions of the social and physical environment with the organism's need to conserve its structural systems.

It would be hard to overemphasize the importance of regarding Piaget as a genetic epistemologist rather than as a psychologist. Each time the writer has attempted to present Piaget's work to psychologists and educators he has had to parry questions about individual differences, motivation, and learning.

What is disturbing about such questions is that they presuppose that Piaget should be concerned with properly psychological issues. One is reminded at such times of those book reviewers who criticize an author for the book he did not write rather than for the one he did write. For the kinds of questions Piaget is concerned with, individual differences, motivation, and learning are largely irrelevant. Piaget is concerned with those structures which, if they hold true for the individual, also hold true for the species. He does not deny that individual differences, motivation, and learning may affect the acquisition of these structures. What he does deny is that such factors affect their identification and it is their identification with which he is primarily concerned. Once identified, the successive forms of these structures can be compared, to arrive at an explication of their genesis. This again can be done on a purely formal basis without specific reference to psychological determinants.

There is no question, of course, that Piaget's work has many important implications for psychology and for education. But this is not the same as saying that the work itself is essentially psychological or pedagogical. Such a contention would be tantamount to saying that Freud was an anthropologist because his work had implications for anthropology or that Darwin was a theologian because his work had implications for theology. The fact that psychology and education can profit so much from Piaget's contribution should not be transformed into the demand that he *be* a psychologist or an educator. Such a demand is particularly shortsighted in view of the fact that Piaget's contribution is so great largely *because* of, rather than in spite of, his being neither psychologist nor educator.

Piaget's genetic epistemology did not emerge full-grown but evolved in the course of more than forty years of intensive and extensive research. This research had three more or less distinct phases. During the first period—marked by the publication of five books (Piaget, 1948, 1951 [a], 1951 [b], 1951 [c], 1952 [b])—Piaget sought, at least in part, to find the parallels between the thought of children and the philosophical systems created by thinkers of antiquity. The aim was not to demonstrate recapitulation—the doctrine that the mind of the child recapitulates that of the race (e.g., Hall, 1908)—but rather to demonstrate the partial constancy of cognitive structuring across long time periods. If the pre-Socratics created a philosophical system around ideas implicit in the thinking of modern-day children, then it is reasonable to suppose that, as children, the pre-Socratics had similar ideas which, as adults, they proceeded to elaborate into a comprehensive philosophy. Such parallels between the thought of antiquity and the implicit world views of today's children constituted some evidence for a constancy of modes of conceptualization which, at least in children, are relatively independent of historicultural conditions.

Although Piaget's work was not carried out in protest to the extreme environmentalism that dominated social scientific thinking during the first decades of this century (his work was rather a protest against armchair epistemology), it did challenge the all-nurture view of child development. In the first place, once it was demonstrated that the child constructed ideas about the world quite different from those entertained by his parents and teachers, a rigid environmentalism had to give way. Secondly, the parallel between the notions constructed by children and those maintained in antiquity was further evidence for the role of genetically determined structures in the acquisition of knowledge. Finally, the fact that the child's spontaneously arrived at notions about the world which were erroneous from the adult point of view meant that the acquisition of knowledge was a more complex process than had hitherto been assumed. In the light of Piaget's studies, the growth of knowledge could no longer be regarded as a simple learning process but had, instead, to be conceived as a giving up of erroneous ideas for more correct ones or as a transformation of these ideas into higher-level, more adequate conceptions. In short, these studies suggested that mental growth was not determined entirely by the unfolding of innate structures nor entirely by the influence of the environment but rather by the constant interaction of these two factors.

During the second phase of his work (marked by three books, 1951 [d], 1952 [c], 1954) Piaget sought to trace in detail the origins of the structures of knowing to the sensorimotor coordinations of infants—in this case his own three children. In these brilliant studies Piaget demonstrated his genius for careful observation, always guided by theoretical considerations which rendered what might have been banal behavior into significant evidence for the development of cognitive structure. As a result of these studies, Piaget was able to demonstrate the infantile forerunners of both the form and content of adult thought.

In the third phase of his work (marked by all the publications since about 1940), Piaget traced the development of logico-mathematical thought from early childhood through adolescence. This period, which continues up until the present day, is characterized by an increasing formalization and systematization of the theoretical considerations sprinkled liberally throughout his previous work. The emphasis during this period, as during the preceding phases, continues to be epistemological. This was particularly evident with the foundation, ten years ago, of the International Center for Genetic Epistemology at Geneva. It is to the development of this Center that Piaget has devoted a large portion of his not inconsiderable energies and administrative talents. Piaget's many allusions to work done in the Center in all of his recent writings suggest that its foundation is a matter of great personal pride and satisfaction to him.

The fact that genetic epistemology has a history must then be taken into account when reading Piaget. Over the years there have been changes in emphasis, conceptualization, and terminology, so that if one speaks of Piaget's work, the date becomes a relevant variable. In his early work, for example, Piaget leaned heavily on social role-taking as the mediator of cognitive development, whereas in the recent work equilibration has come to be his dominant explanatory process. Like any scientific discipline, genetic epistemology is an open, changing system which has both a history and a future.

A third factor that has to be considered in reading Piaget is that genetic epistemology is a multidisciplinary science. It is probably not possible to answer the question as to whether Piaget became a genetic epistemologist because of his diverse scientific interests or whether these interests were aroused by his conception of a genetic epistemology. What is clear is that an informed reading of Piaget requires an acquaintance with biology, physics, logic, and philosophy as a bare minimum. In an age of increasing specialization, Piaget requires his readers to leap established scientific boundaries and to look at the child's behavior from many different points of view.

In summary, three considerations must be kept in mind when reading Piaget. First of all, he has created a new discipline with its own problems, methods and theory. Secondly, genetic epistemology has a history and a future, which is to say it is a growing and evolving system. This means that Piaget's writings can be correctly evaluated only within a relative historical context and never from an absolute, once-and-for-all point of view. Finally, genetic epistemology is broad, rather than narrow, in scope and encompasses many different disciplines, so it cannot be reduced to any one of them.

Although Piaget's genetic epistemology has evolved over the years since he first began his investigations, three themes persist and provide the continuity amid change that characterizes all of his work. These three themes are logic, relativity, and dialectics, and each must be considered in somewhat greater detail.

Logic. Within Piaget's genetic epistemology, logic plays a central role. Logic is the genotypic link between the phenotypic diversity of the sciences. If logic is inherent in the mind, in biological processes, and in the laws that govern the physical world, then it must be the key to man's understanding of nature. It is thus the presence of logical operations in the child which permits him to reconstruct and understand the physical, social, and biological worlds. If logic is inherent in psychic activity from the start of life this does not, however, preclude its evolution in the course of individual development. The logic to be discerned in the behavior of the infant is much more primitive and much less systematic than that observed in the preschool or elementary school child. It is only in adolescents that a true, or formal, logical system, comparable to that constructed by logicians, develops. But if logic is taken in the broad sense to mean a set of actions that obey logic-like rules, such as transitivity, then it can be said that at all age levels behavior manifests some form of logic.

Piaget's recognition of logic as the mediating factor in the construction of knowledge was probably attributable, at least in part, to his teacher at the University of Neuchâtel, Arnold Reymond. It was Reymond, the philosopher logician, who pointed out to Piaget the relationship between Aristotelian logic and biology and hence ended Piaget's infatuation with the Bergsonian dualism between the vital and the logico-mathematical. It was Reymond, too, who showed Piaget the general philosophical and scientific implications which resided in any particular and concrete issue.

In his own work Piaget has tried to construct a logic of mental operations with psychological validity. Unlike Boole (1951), who in a sense attempted to do the same, Piaget built his logic of operations upon what he observed when children at different age levels were confronted with tasks that required reasoning for their solution. Although this genetic logic (first attempted by Baldwin, 1906–08) has been criticized by logicians, it is nevertheless the first successful attempt to construct a logical model of thought based upon experiment rather than armchair speculation. If, as Piaget seems to have shown, all intelligence and thought manifest a logical structure, then they are at one with the biological and social realities which manifest a like structure. Logic is thus the bedrock upon which any epistemology must be built.

Relativity. Scientists, no less than the man in the street, have their own matinee idols. In the 1920s Einstein—whose most widely read presentation of his theories of relativity was published in 1917—quickly became the model of what a scientist should be. Although Einstein's theory of relativity was not the first such theory in physics, it nonetheless appealed, like some pleasing tune, to layman and scientist alike. For Piaget the theory of relativity had special allure. If, as Einstein had shown, conceptual judgments were always relative to the position of the observer making those judgments, then the observer could never be left out in the construction of concepts. This contention reinforced a pre-established Piaget conviction—derived from Kant and perhaps from Marx—that reality always involved a subjective element, in the sense that it was always, at least in part, a projection or externalization of thought or action.

Epistemological relativism permeates Piaget's thinking about the construction of reality. Even the simplest environmental influence or stimulation is never passively received and registered, but is always acted upon. The infant who brings everything he touches toward his mouth is constructing a world of things to be sucked and thus organizes the world in terms of his own actions. To deny that there is a psychological reality without the intervention of the subject's activity is not to deny the separate existence of an external world. All that such a denial means is that all knowledge is mediate (or "mediated," as we say today) rather than immediate (or copied directly).

At this point a concrete example of the evidence for epistemological relativism might help to clarify this position. If a child of five is asked to match six pennies spaced out in a row with a like number from a nearby pile, he can do so without difficulty. Once the two rows are in one-to-one correspondence the child says that both rows have the same number. If one then moves the pennies in one row farther apart than those in the other, the five-year-old says that one of the rows has more pennies than the other. When the latter problem is presented to a seven-year-old, however, the reaction is quite different. In the first place, the child regards the question as rather stupid and replies that of course the two rows have the same number since nothing was added or taken away or since spreading them apart does not alter their number. The point of this illustration is that the older child takes as self-evident, or *a priori*, what only a few short years before he did not know existed! *Once a concept is constructed, it is immediately externalized so that it appears to the subject as a perceptually given property of the object and independent of the subject's own mental activity.* The tendency of mental activities to become automatized and for their results to be perceived as external to the subject is what leads to the conviction that there is a reality independent of thought. It is not surprising, under these circumstances, that the copy theory, as Boring (1950) said, dies hard. The absolute separation between mind and matter is an illusion, but one that can be overcome only by examination of the development of thought in the child.

Dialectics. As has been indicated, logic represents the factor common to mental, biological, and physical science, whereas relativity describes the relation between mind and reality. The third factor, dialectics, expresses the dynamic of mental growth and the acquisition of knowledge. Mental growth is clearly determined by three major sets of factors: maturation, physical experience, and social experience. Since, however, these factors interact in a complex fashion, no one of them can itself explain the nature of their activity as a whole. It is for this reason that Piaget felt the need to introduce a fourth factor, equilibration, as an overriding factor that determines the mode of interaction of the other three.

The principle of equilibration which regulates the interaction of maturational and environmental influences is essentially dialectical in nature. At each level of development there are two poles of activity: changes in the structure of the organism in response to environmental intrusion (accommodation), and changes in the intruding stimuli due to the existing structure (assimilation). These two poles of activity constitute a sort of thesis and antithesis whose eventual synthesis is effected by a process of equilibration. In practice, this means that a new structural system is evolved such that each new intrusion can be incorporated without either a change in the structure or a change in the stimulus—in other words, so that the integrity of the internal and external systems is conserved.

As Piaget is at pains to point out in one of the essays in this book, an equilibrated system is never static and closed but always mobile and open. Each new level of mental equilibrium prepares for a new disequilibrium, just as each state of biological equilibrium (say, satiation) is preparatory to a new disequilibrium (say, hunger). On the mental plane, each new level of conceptualization establishes a new equilibrium but also opens the subject to new forms of information and new possibilities of contradiction. The same is true in science. The notion of evolution, for example, explained the variations among species and produced a new equilibrium in biological thinking, while at the same time it created a disequilibrium in the theological system of thought. On a more psychological level, Festinger's (1957) theory of cognitive dissonance could be easily expressed in terms of equilibration between contradictory beliefs. For Piaget, equilibration is, at all levels of analysis, the dynamic of cognitive change without which the effects of maturation, physical experience, and social experience cannot be understood or explained.

Logic, relativity, and dialectics are, then, the three major themes of Piaget's genetic epistemology. It is logic which provides the common genotype of the mental, biological, and physical sciences. Relativity expresses the nature of the mind-reality relationship, while dialectic equilibration provides the dynamic or growth principle which governs both the acquisition of knowledge and the structures necessary for this acquisition.

The studies brought together in the present volume span a period of almost a quarter of a century. As such they reflect both Piaget's unvarying preoccupation and his evolving conceptualizations. While there is considerable repetition between these studies, each nonetheless highlights a different facet of Piaget's thinking.

In the first paper, entitled "The Mental Development of the Child," Piaget provides a comprehensive overview of his position on psychological development as he viewed it in 1940. Of particular note in this study is Piaget's attempt to deal with personality development and affectivity (*affectivité*), which for French-speaking psychologists corresponds to the motivational-emotional aspects of the person. Although Piaget has generally avoided this area, he does take it up in the present study. Not surprisingly, he is less original in this domain than in the cognitive sphere, and his ideas on these topics are often similar to those that have been proposed by others. These parallels are pointed out in editorial footnotes which accompany the text.

It might be well, however, to try to put down what seems to be Piaget's position with respect to affectivity. By and large, Piaget would seem to be a double-aspect theorist. From this point of view, motivation and cognitive structure are not separate entities but are rather different sides of the same thing. In other words, every cognitive structure can be said to embody its own dynamic. Once a structure is present, utilizing it becomes a need which is satisfied through exercise or—in non-Piagetian terms—through function pleasure. Accordingly, cognitive structures do not need to be energized by drives, appetites, or other extraneous motivators since they are self-activating. The cognitive systems termed "personality" and "self" do not differ in this respect. If they differ from other cognitive systems—such as those dealing with the physical world—then it is in terms of their content, not their mode of operation. The self and the personality are simply those conceptual systems concerned with personal and interpersonal realities. At each stage of development such systems are governed by the same laws of organization that rule the whole of mental life at that period.

For Piaget, the self and personality correspond to different stages of development. During childhood, the self system evolves from one which is entirely egocentric, or self-centered, to one which can take the other person's point of view into account when making judgments. In personal and interpersonal matters, the development of the self system reveals the same progressive objectification which occurs with respect to physical reality. Personality, however, does not emerge until adolescence and the appearance of formal operations which enable the young person to form life plans that project his activity into the future and which go beyond personal concerns and have consequences for society as a whole. Just as formal operations build upon and incorporate the concrete operational structures, so does personality build upon and incorporate the self system. In some ways Piaget's concept of personality parallels Erikson's (1963) concept of ego identity, the sense of personal wholeness which is also a construction of adolescence. For both Piaget and Erikson, the person does not become a true individual or personality until he has integrated his thoughts and feelings about himself into a total life perspective which expands beyond personal interest to the whole of mankind.

The second essay, "The Thought of the Young Child," is of interest for two different reasons. First of all, while it covers much the same material as the first essay, it reveals considerable refinement and sophistication of research and theory over the earlier work. The second, and perhaps more important, reason is that it clearly demonstrates Piaget's overriding epistemological concerns. Given a chance to say what the implications of his work are, Piaget makes clear that he regards it as propaedeutic to other sciences. Piaget says that his work demonstrates at least three things: (a) the differences between adult and child thought; (b) the value of a genetic model for psychological explication in general; and (c) the value of genetic research for resolving problems raised by the philosophy of science.

Of particular note is the fact that Piaget nowhere points to the practical implications of his work. Indeed he seems to feel that a solid foundation of genetic research and theory is necessary before useful practical implications can be drawn. If one looks carefully through Piaget's writings one seldom, if ever, finds an attempt to deal with concrete problems of pedagogy or child rearing. This is an important point. Some educators have engaged in certain teaching practices in the name of Piaget. What should always be made clear in such cases is that it is the educator's interpretation of Piaget which is being utilized and not Piaget's own ideas about educational practice. If Piaget has such, he seldom voices them.

Piaget's third essay, "Language and Thought from the Genetic Point of View," is of considerable importance because it is one of Piaget's few systematic attempts to deal with the relation between the development of thought and language. Piaget's general position seems to be that thought can neither be reduced to language nor explained by it. Thought cannot be reduced to language, since, when language is absent, as in the case of the deaf, thought can still be shown to exist. Likewise, thought cannot be explained by language because the linguistic conquest of rational tasks follows, rather than proceeds, their resolution on the plane of action. More particularly, thought and language seem to have different origins. Thought derives from the abstraction of one's own actions upon things. Ordering objects, putting them into groups, transforming them in multiple ways by motor manipulations provide the basis for those abstractions which become mental operations. Language, on the other hand, is derived from experiences which are not a product of the child's own activity but are rather imitations of patterns provided by adults. It is this difference in origin which accounts for the fundamental duality between thought and language.

This is not to say, however, that thought and language are independent of one another but only that they cannot be reduced or explained by one another. Once language appears, it is in constant interaction with thought. In a sense, language is to thought what mathematics is to physics, a tool and a handmaiden rather than a master. Like mathematics, language facilitates the expansion of thought and adds to its mobility. With the aid of language, thought can do much more than it would otherwise be capable of doing. Yet this fact should not lead to the identification of thought with language, for the reasons given above.

In "The Role of the Concept of Psychological Equilibrium in Psychological Explication" Piaget deals with a theme which has long dominated his thinking and which was lightly touched upon in our earlier discussion. Piaget argues that some form of equilibration theory has appeared in every comprehensive attempt to explain human behavior. With respect to development, equilibration provides the laws of interaction for the other determinants of behavior: maturation and social and physical experience. Such a view, however, presents numerous difficulties which Piaget takes up and answers. In addition, he demonstrates how equilibration works on the perceptual plane and in so doing gives a brief summary of his complex perceptual theory.

It is perhaps worthwhile to mention the similarities and differences between Piaget's notion of equilibration and Gestalt theory. Like Gestalt psychologists, Piaget assumes that the laws which govern the parts (in this case maturation and experience) cannot explain the laws of their interaction and that these laws of the whole form a separate system, namely equilibration. Piaget differs from the Gestalt point of view in that he believes that the laws of the whole have a genesis and are developmental, rather than being relatively fixed characteristics of the nervous system. In addition, Piaget holds that, from a logical and epistemological point of view, perception is secondary to rational intelligence and that the two form distinct systems. Gestalt psychologists, on the contrary, often seem to make perception primary and to reduce intelligence to the laws of perceptual functioning.

The general significance of Piaget's equilibration theory has yet to be generally recognized. It is probably fair to say that most psychological theories are additive or multiplicative, in the sense that they assume interacting factors summate or multiply to produce their effects. Piaget, on the other hand, assumes that the laws of interaction are "emergent," in the sense that they are not reducible to any simple arithmetic combination of the individual factors involved.

Piaget's fifth essay, "Problems of Genetic Psychology," is likely to give the reader a surprise. At one point in the discussion Piaget seems to argue for the inheritance of acquired characteristics. This argument, however, must be taken in context. Piaget is really arguing the point that no structure is entirely innate or acquired and that what might seem to be innate can always be traced back to some kind of experience—of the individual or species—just as any acquired structure can be shown to be relative to structures which the organism already had on hand. Put differently, Piaget is trying to point out the futility of trying to separate nature and nurture in the formation of structures and is not revealing a hidden Lamarckianism.

The sixth essay, "Genesis and Structure," is still another approach to the same problem but this time in terms of the laws which govern growth and those which govern the organization of structures. Again, the attempt to trace the laws of structure to those of growth, or vice versa, is fruitless since the regress is infinite. Every structure has a genesis and all genesis proceeds from structure, so that their explication cannot come from themselves but requires the introduction of a new factor. Not surprisingly, this *tertium quid* is equilibration.

In summary, these essays would seem to place Piaget's concerns in proper perspective. He is not fundamentally a child psychologist concerned with practical issues of child growth and development. He is rather, first and foremost, a genetic epistemologist concerned with the nature of knowledge and with the structures and processes by which it is acquired. In this connection, his overriding concern is to show that in all discussions of development of knowledge, the roles of maturation and experience cannot be fully understood without consideration of an additional encompassing factor, namely, equilibration.

David Elkind

Contents

EDITOR'S INTRODUCTION   v

GLOSSARY   xxii

PART ONE

I. The Mental Development of the Child   3

  1. The Neonate and the Infant   8

  2. Early Childhood from Two to Seven Years   17

    A. THE SOCIALIZATION OF ACTION   18

    B. THE GENESIS OF THOUGHT   22

    C. INTUITION   29

    D. THE AFFECTIVE LIFE   33

  3. Childhood from Seven to Twelve Years   38

    A. THE PROGRESS AND SOCIALIZATION OF BEHAVIOR   38

    B. THE PROGRESS OF THOUGHT   41

    C. THE RATIONAL OPERATIONS   48

    D. AFFECTIVITY, WILL, AND MORAL FEELINGS   54

  4. Adolescence   60

    A. THOUGHT AND ITS OPERATIONS   61

    B. THE AFFECTIVITY OF THE PERSONALITY IN THE SOCIAL WORLD OF ADULTS   64

PART TWO

II. The Thought of the Young Child   77

  1. The Child and the Adult   78

2. The Cognitive Structures   81
3. Psychology and Genetic Epistemology   83
III. *Language and Thought from the Genetic Point of View*   88
1. Thought and the Symbolic Function   88
2. Language and the "Concrete" Logical Operations   92
3. Language and Propositional Logic   94
IV. *The Role of the Concept of Equilibrium in Psychological Explication*   100
1. The Explicative Role of the Concept of Equilibrium   102
2. Models of Equilibrium   107
3. Conclusion   113
V. *Problems of Genetic Psychology*   116
1. Innateness and Acquisition   117
2. The Problem of the Necessity Proper to the Logical Structures   120
3. The Development of Perception   131
VI. *Genesis and Structure in the Psychology of Intelligence*   143
1. Historical Background   144
2. Genesis Emanates from a Structure and Culminates in a Structure   147
3. Every Structure Has a Genesis   149
4. Equilibrium   150
5. Example of Logico-Mathematical Structures   152
6. Case Study   154

BIBLIOGRAPHICAL REFERENCES   159
BIOGRAPHICAL NOTE   163
INDEX OF NAMES   165
SUBJECT INDEX   167

Translators' Note

TRANSLATION IS ALWAYS a compromise between fidelity to the author's style and consideration for the reader's patience. In the case of Piaget, we have tried to simplify his often complex sentence structure without at the same time losing the Piaget flavor. At many points the translation is loose rather than literal, both to avoid Gallicisms and to ease the flow of language. In choosing English words to match Piaget's terminology we have, wherever possible, used the same terms as those employed in previous translations of his works. Hopefully, this will provide continuity and avoid confusion.

Editor's Note

IN THE ORIGINAL TEXT, particularly in the first paper, Piaget makes many references to the writings of a variety of authors without citing the particular works he had in mind. On the basis of the content of the discussion, the Editor has tried to trace the relevant work and to provide the appropriate reference. Every attempt was made to keep editorial notes to a minimum, and no effort was made to explicate Piaget's logic or his theory of perception, since such explication would require full-length treatment. Readers wishing to go into these subjects in more detail will find abundant references in the text to works which give comprehensive treatment to these matters.

Glossary

Egocentrism Piaget uses this term to mean the child's inability to take another's point of view. It is not a perjorative term with respect to the child since the child does not take another's point of view because *he cannot* as opposed to the egocentric adult who can take another's point of view but *will not*.

Equilibration An overriding principle of mental development in the sense that all mental growth progresses toward ever more complex and stable levels of organization.

Intuition A form of thought in which judgments regarding physical reality are made on the basis of perception rather than reason.

Schemata In the specific sense schemata are the senori-motor equivalents of concepts in that they permit the infant to deal economically with different objects of the same class and with different states of the same object. In the general sense schemata are the structures at any level of mental development. Piaget uses the term schemata in both senses.

Structure A mental system or totality whose principles of activity are different from those of the parts which make it up.

PART

One

CHAPTER 1

The Mental Development of the Child [1]

♫ THE PSYCHOLOGICAL DEVELOPMENT that starts at birth and terminates in adulthood is comparable to organic growth. Like the latter, it consists essentially of activity directed toward equilibrium. Just as the body evolves toward a relatively stable level characterized by the completion of the growth process and by organ maturity, so mental life can be conceived as evolving toward a final form of equilibrium represented by the adult mind. In a sense, development is a progressive equilibration from a lesser to a higher state of equilibrium. From the point of view of intelligence, it is easy to contrast the relative instability and incoherence of childhood ideas with the systemization of adult reason. With respect to the affective life, it has frequently been noted how extensively emotional equilibrium increases with age. Social relations also obey the same law of gradual stabilization.

An essential difference between the life of the body and that of the mind must nonetheless be stressed if the dynamism inherent in the reality of the mind is to be respected. The final form of equilibrium reached through organic growth is more static and, above all, more unstable than the equilibrium toward which mental development strives, so that no sooner has ascending evolution terminated than a regressive evolution automatically starts, leading to old age. Certain psychological functions that depend closely on the physical condition of the body follow an analogous curve. Visual acuity, for example, is at a maximum toward the end of childhood, only to diminish subsequently; and many other perceptual processes are regulated by the same law. By contrast, the higher functions of intelligence and affectivity tend toward a "mobile equilibrium." The more mobile it is, the more stable it is, so that the termination of growth, in healthy minds, by no means marks the beginning of decline but rather permits progress that in no sense contradicts inner equilibrium.

It is thus in terms of equilibrium that we shall try to describe the evolution of the child and the adolescent. From this point of view, mental development is a continuous construction comparable to the erection of a vast building that becomes more solid with each addition. Alternatively, and perhaps more appropriately, it may be likened to the assembly of a subtle mechanism that goes through gradual phases of adjustment in which the individual pieces become more supple and mobile as the equilibrium of the mechanism as a whole becomes more stable. We must, however, introduce an important distinction between two complementary aspects of the process of equilibration. This is the distinction between the variable structures that define the successive states of equilibrium and a certain constant functioning that assures the transition from any one state to the following one.

There is sometimes a striking similarity between the reactions of the child and the adult, as, for example, when the child is sure of what he wants and acts as adults do with respect to their own special interests. At other times there is a world of difference—in games, for example, or in the manner of reasoning. From a functional point of view, i.e., if we take into consideration the general motives of behavior and thought, there are constant functions common to all ages. At all levels of development, action presupposes a precipitating factor: a physiological, affective, or intellectual need. (In the latter case, the need appears in the guise of a question or a problem.) At all levels, intelligence seeks to understand or to explain, etc. However, while the functions of interest, explanation, etc., are common to all developmental stages, that is to say, are "invariable" as far as the functions themselves are concerned, it is nonetheless true that "interests" (as opposed to "interest") vary considerably from one mental level to another, and that the particular explanations (as opposed to the function of explaining) are of a very different nature, depending on the degree of intellectual development. In addition to the constant functions, there are the variable structures. An analysis of these progressive forms of successive equilibrium highlights the differences from one behavioral level to another, all the way from the elementary behavior of the neonate through adolescence.

The variable structures—motor or intellectual on the one hand and affective on the other—are the organizational forms of mental activity. They are organized along two dimensions—intrapersonal and social (interpersonal). For greater clarity we shall distinguish six stages or periods of development which mark the appearance of these successively constructed structures:

1) The reflex or hereditary stage, at which the first instinctual nutritional drives and the first emotions appear.

2) The stage of the first motor habits and of the first organized percepts, as well as of the first differentiated emotions.

3) The stage of sensorimotor or practical intelligence (prior to language), of elementary affective organization, and of the first external affective fixations. These first three stages constitute the infancy period—from birth till the age of one and a half to two years—i.e., the period prior to the development of language and thought as such.

4) The stage of intuitive intelligence, of spontaneous interpersonal feelings, and of social relationships in which the child is subordinate to the adult (ages two to seven years, or "early childhood").

5) The stage of concrete intellectual operations (the beginning of logic) and of moral and social feelings of cooperation (ages seven to eleven or twelve, or "middle childhood").

6) The stage of abstract intellectual operations, of the formation of the personality, and of affective and intellectual entry into the society of adults (adolescence).

Each of these stages is characterized by the appearance of original structures whose construction distinguishes it from previous stages. The essentials of these successive constructions exist at subsequent stages in the form of substructures onto which new characteristics have been built. It follows that in the adult each stage through which he has passed corresponds to a given level in the total hierarchy of behavior. But at each stage there are also temporary and secondary characteristics that are modified by subsequent development as a function of the need for better organization. Each stage thus constitutes a particular form of equilibrium as a function of its characteristic structures, and mental evolution is effectuated in the direction of an ever-increasing equilibrium.

We know which functional mechanisms are common to all stages. In an absolutely general way (not only in comparing one stage with the following but also in comparing each item of behavior that is part of that stage with ensuing behavior), one can say that all action—that is to say, all movement, all thought, or all emotion—responds to a need. Neither the child nor the adult executes any external or even entirely internal act unless impelled by a motive; this motive can always be translated into a need (an elementary need, an interest, a question, etc.).

As Claparède [1951] has shown, a need is always a manifestation of disequilibrium: there is need when something either outside ourselves or within us (physically or mentally) is changed and behavior has to be adjusted as a function of this change. For example, hunger or fatigue will provoke a search for nourishment or rest; encountering an external object will lead to a need to play, which in turn has practical ends, or it leads to a question or a theoretical problem. A casual word will excite the need to imitate, to sympathize, or will engender reserve or opposition if it conflicts with some interest of our own. Conversely, action terminates when a need is satisfied, that is to say, when equilibrium is re-established between the new factor that has provoked the need and the mental organization that existed prior to the introduction of this factor. Eating or sleeping, playing or reaching a goal, replying to a question or resolving a problem, imitating successfully, establishing an affective tie, or maintaining one's point of view are all satisfactions that, in the preceding examples, will put an end to the particular behavior aroused by the need. At any given moment, one can thus say, action is disequilibrated by the transformations that arise in the external or internal world, and each new behavior consists not only in re-establishing equilibrium but also in moving toward a more stable equilibrium than that which preceded the disturbance.

Human action consists of a continuous and perpetual mechanism of readjustment or equilibration. For this reason, in these initial phases of construction, the successive mental structures that engender development can be considered as so many progressive forms of equilibrium, each of which is an advance upon its predecessor. It must be understood, however, that this functional mechanism, general though it may be, does not explain the content or the structure of the various needs, since each of them is related to the organization of the particular stage that is being considered. For example, the sight of the same object will occasion very different questions in the small child who is still incapable of classification from those of the older child whose ideas are more extensive and systematic. The interests of a child at any given moment depend on the system of ideas he has acquired plus his affective inclinations, and he tends to fulfill his interests in the direction of greater equilibrium.

Before examining the details of development we must try to find that which is common to the needs and interests present at all ages. One can say, in regard to this, that all needs tend first of all to incorporate things and people into the subject's own activity, i.e., to "assimilate" the external world into the structures that have already been constructed, and secondly to readjust these structures as a function of subtle transformations, i.e., to "accommodate" them to external objects. From this point of view, all mental life, as indeed all organic life, tends progressively to assimilate the surrounding environment. This incorporation is effected thanks to the structures or psychic organs whose scope of action becomes more and more extended. Initially, perception and elementary movement (prehension, etc.) are concerned with objects that are close and viewed statically; then later, memory and practical intelligence permit the representation of earlier states of the object as well as the anticipation of their future states resulting from as yet unrealized transformations. Still later intuitive thought reinforces these two abilities. Logical intelligence in the guise of concrete operations and ultimately of abstract deduction terminates this evolution by making the subject master of events that are far distant in space and time. At each of these levels the mind fulfills the same function, which is to incorporate the universe to itself, but the nature of assimilation varies, i.e., the successive modes of incorporation evolve from those of perception and movement to those of the higher mental operations.

In assimilating objects, action and thought must accommodate to these objects; they must adjust to external variation. The balancing of the processes of assimilation and accommodation may be called "adaptation." Such is the general form of psychological equilibrium, and the progressive organization of mental development appears to be simply an ever more precise adaptation to reality. We shall now examine these stages of adaptation more closely.

1. THE NEONATE AND THE INFANT

The period that extends from birth to the acquisition of language is marked by an extraordinary development of the mind.

Its importance is sometimes underestimated because it is not accompanied by words that permit a step-by-step pursuit of the progress of intelligence and the emotions, as is the case later on. This early mental development nonetheless determines the entire course of psychological evolution. In fact, it is no less than a conquest by perception and movement of the entire practical universe that surrounds the small child. At eighteen months to two years this "sensorimotor assimilation" of the immediate external world effects a miniature Copernican revolution. At the starting point of this development the neonate grasps everything to himself—or, in more precise terms, to his own body—whereas at the termination of this period, i.e., when language and thought begin, he is for all practical purposes but one element or entity among others in a universe that he has gradually constructed himself, and which hereafter he will experience as external to himself.

Step by step, we shall describe the stages of this Copernican revolution in its twofold aspect of intelligence and nascent affective life. With respect to the development of intelligence, we have already cited three stages between birth and the end of the first period: the reflex stage, the stage of the organization of percepts and habits, and the stage of sensorimotor intelligence itself.

At birth, mental life is limited to the exercise of reflex apparatuses, i.e., of hereditarily determined sensory and motor coordinations that correspond to instinctual needs, such as nutrition. To the extent that these reflexes bear on the behavior that will play a role in subsequent psychological development, they have none of the mechanical passivity that might be attributed to them. On the contrary, from the very outset, they manifest genuine activity, which is the best evidence for the existence of precocious sensorimotor assimilation. The sucking reflexes, for example, become refined, and the neonate sucks better after one or two weeks than during the first days. At a somewhat later age, these reflexes lead to practical discriminations and recognitions that are easily observed. Still later, and most important, these reflexes give rise to a kind of generalization of activity. The infant is not content to suck only when he nurses; he also sucks at random. He sucks his fingers when he encounters them, then whatever object may be presented fortuitously, and finally he coordinates the movement of his arms with the sucking until he is able to introduce his thumb into his mouth systematically, sometimes as early as the second month. In short, the infant assimilates a part of his universe to his sucking to the degree that his initial behavior can be described by saying that for him the world is essentially a thing to be sucked. In short order, this same universe will also become a thing to be looked at, to listen to, and, as soon as his own movements allow, to shake.

The diverse exercise of reflexes, which is the forerunner of mental assimilation, rapidly becomes complicated as it is integrated into habits and organized percepts. We are then at the threshold of new behaviors acquired with the aid of experience. Systematic thumb-sucking belongs to this second stage, as does the turning of the head in the direction of a sound or the following of a moving object, etc. From the perceptual point of view, from the time a child starts to smile (from the fifth week on), he recognizes certain persons as distinct from others, etc. We must not, however, assume that he conceptualizes a person or even an object. Persons and objects are tangible and animated apparitions which he recognizes as such, but this proves nothing with respect to their substantiality, nor as to the dissociation between the self and the external universe. Between three and six months (usually at around four and a half months) the infant begins to grasp what he sees; this capacity for prehension and then for manipulation broadens his potentiality for acquiring new habits.

At the outset of life there is only one kind of system, which might be called sensorimotor schemata. These elementary sensorimotor schemata are then differentiated into new motor systems (habits) and new perceptual organizations. The point of departure for this differentiation is always a reflex cycle. This cycle does not, however, merely repeat itself. It incorporates new elements and together with them constitutes broader organized totalities by means of progressive differentiation. Subsequently, it suffices that the infant's random movements fortuitously produce something interesting (interesting because it can be assimilated into a prior schema) for him to repeat these new movements immediately. This "circular reaction," as it has been called,[2] plays an essential role in sensorimotor development and represents a more advanced form of assimilation.

We now come to the third stage, which is even more important to the course of development: the stage of practical and sensorimotor intelligence itself. Intelligence actually appears well before language, that is to say, well before internal thought, which presupposes the use of verbal signs (internalized language). It is an entirely practical intelligence based on the manipulation of objects; in place of words and concepts it uses percepts and movements organized into "action schemata." For example, to grab a stick in order to draw up a remote object is an act of intelligence (and a fairly late developing one at that: about eighteen months). Here, an instrument, the means to an end, is coordinated with a pre-established goal. In order to discover this means, the subject must first understand the relationship between the stick and the objective. A more precocious act of intelligence consists in bringing the objective closer by means of pulling the support on which it is resting. This occurs toward the end of the first year. Many other examples could be cited.

Let us see how these acts of intelligence are constructed. Two kinds of factors are involved. First of all, early behavior becomes increasingly elaborated and differentiated to the point where the infant acquires sufficient behavioral facility for him to notice the results of his actions. In these "circular reactions" the baby is not content merely to reproduce movements and gestures that have led to an interesting effect. He varies them intentionally in order to study the results of these variations and thus gives himself over to true explorations or to "experiments in order to see." This is exemplified by the behavior of the twelve-month-old child who throws objects on the ground in one direction or another in order to see how and where they fall.

Secondly, the "action schemata" constructed at the previous stage and multiplied through new experimental behaviors become capable of coordinating with one another through a process of reciprocal assimilation. This process is analogous to what will occur later in the ideas or concepts of thought itself. In effect, an action that can be repeated and generalized to a new situation might be thought of as a kind of sensorimotor concept. For example, a baby presented with a new object successively incorporates it into each of his "action schemata" (shaking it, stroking it, balancing it, etc.), as though he could come to know the object by perceiving how it is used. (At five or six years children still define concepts by starting with the words, "It is for": a table "is for writing on," etc.) The sensorimotor assimilation at this stage is comparable to what will later be an assimilation of reality by ideas and thought. It is natural, then, that these various action schemata should become assimilated with one another, i.e., coordinated so that some serve as a goal for action as a whole, while others serve as a means. This coordination of the action schemata is comparable to, but more mobile and supple than, the coordination of the preceding stage. It introduces practical intelligence itself.

The result of this intellectual development is in effect to transform the representation of things to the point of completely changing or inverting the subject's initial position with respect to them. At the outset of mental evolution there is no definite differentiation between the self and the external world, i.e., impressions that are experienced and perceived are not attached to a personal consciousness sensed as a "self," nor to objects conceived as external to the self. They simply exist in a dissociated block or are spread out on the same plane, which is neither internal nor external but midway between these two poles. These opposing poles will only gradually become differentiated. It follows that, because of this primitive lack of dissociation, everything that is perceived is centered on the subject's own activity. The self is at the center of reality to begin with for the very reason that it is not aware of itself, while the external world will become objectified to the degree that the self builds itself as a function of subjective or internal activity. In other words, consciousness starts with an unconscious and integral egocentricity, whereas the progress of sensorimotor intelligence leads to the construction of an objective universe in which the subject's own body is an element among others and with which the internal life, localized in the subject's own body, is contrasted.

Four fundamental processes characterize the intellectual revolution that is accomplished during the first two years of existence. These are the construction of the categories of the object, of space, of causality, and of time.[3] All four refer, of course, to purely practical or action categories and not as yet to ideas or thinking.

The practical schema of the object is the substantial permanence attributed to sensory pictures. It is the belief that what is seen corresponds to "something" which continues to exist even when one does not perceive it. It is easy to demonstrate that during the first months the infant does not perceive objects in this sense. He recognizes certain familiar sensory pictures, it is true, but the fact that he recognizes them when they are present by no means implies that he can place them when they are no longer within his perceptual field. In particular, he recognizes persons and he knows very well that when he cries he can make his mother return after she has disappeared, but this by no means proves that when he no longer sees her he attributes to her a body existing in space. Actually, when the infant begins to grasp what he sees, he at first shows no search behavior when the toys he wants are covered by a handkerchief. This is so even when he has visually followed what is being done. Later on he will look for the hidden object but without noticing its successive displacements. It is as though each object were part of the configuration as a whole and could not be moved separately. It is only toward the end of the first year that objects are sought out when they leave the perceptual field; this is a criterion for the beginning of the externalization of the material world. In short, the initial absence of substantive objects, followed by the construction of solid and permanent objects, is the first example of the transition from primitive, total egocentricity to the final elaboration of an external universe.

The evolution of practical space is entirely at one with the construction of objects. At the outset there are as many spaces —uncoordinated among themselves—as sensory fields (oral spaces, visual spaces, tactile spaces, etc.), and each one of them is centered on the child's own movements and activity. Visual space, in particular, does not have the same depth at the outset that it will have later on. By the end of the second year, however, a sense of general space has been acquired which includes all the other particular spaces and which is characterized by relationships among objects and between objects and the child's own body. The elaboration of space is essentially derived from the coordination of movements so that there is a direct relationship between the development of a sense of space and of sensorimotor intelligence.

Causality is linked first of all with the child's own activity and his egocentrism. It is the link—which for a long time will seem to the child to be fortuitous—between an empirical result and some action that has brought it about. For example, when an infant pulls at the cords that hang from the top of his crib and the toys also suspended from the top start to shake, he will relate the act of pulling the cords causally with the general effect of movement that ensues. He will henceforth use this causal schema in order to activate anything whatever at a distance. He will pull the cord in order to continue the action of a seesaw he sees two meters away from his crib and in order to prolong a whistling sound he hears at the other end of his room, etc. This kind of magic causality or "magico-phenomenistic" causality demonstrates primitive causal egocentricity. By contrast, in the course of the second year the child recognizes the causal relationships among objects; he can then objectify and spatialize causes.

The objectification of temporal series parallels the development of causality. In short, in all areas we find this kind of Copernican revolution enabling sensorimotor intelligence to extricate the nascent mind from its radical unconscious egocentricity and to place it in a "universe," however practical and however "unreflective" this universe may be.

The evolution of affectivity during the first two years corresponds fairly closely to the evolution of motor and cognitive functions. There is a constant parallel between the affective and intellectual life throughout childhood and adolescence. This statement will seem surprising only if one attempts to dichotomize the life of the mind into emotions and thoughts. But nothing could be more false or superficial. In reality, the element to which we must constantly turn in the analysis of mental life is "behavior" itself, conceived, as we have tried to point out briefly in our introduction, as a re-establishment or strengthening of equilibrium. All behavior presupposes instruments and a technique: movements and intelligence. But all behavior also implies motives and final values (goals): the sentiments. Thus affectivity and intelligence are indissociable and constitute the two complementary aspects of all human behavior.

This being so, it is clear that during the initial stage of reflex techniques there are corresponding elementary instinctive strivings linked with nutrition as well as the kind of affective reflexes that constitute the primary emotions. Recently the relationship between the emotions and the physiological system of attitudes and postures has been shown. The first fears, for example, can be related to losses of equilibrium or to sudden contrasts between a fortuitous event and a preceding attitude.[4]

At the second stage (percepts and habits), as well as at the beginnings of sensorimotor intelligence, there is a corresponding series of elementary emotions or affective percepts linked to the modalities of activity itself: the agreeable or the disagreeable, pleasure and pain, etc., as well as the first realizations of success and failure. To the extent that these affective states depend on action per se and not as yet on awareness of relationships with other people, this level of affectivity attests to a kind of general egocentricity and gives the impression, if one mistakenly attributes a sense of self to the baby, of a kind of love of self and of one's own activity. It is true that the infant begins by being mainly interested in his own body, in its movements, and in the results of his actions. Psychoanalysis has called this elementary stage of affectivity "narcissism," but it is important to understand that it is a narcissism without Narcissus, i.e., without any sense of personal awareness as such.

With the development of intelligence, however, and with the ensuing elaboration of an external universe and especially with the construction of the schema of the "object," a third level of affectivity appears. It is epitomized, in the language of psychoanalysis, by the "object choice," i.e., by the objectivation of the emotions and by their projection onto activities other than those of the self alone. Let us note, first of all, that with the progress of intelligent behavior the emotions linked to activity become differentiated and multiplied: joy and sadness linked to success and failure of intentional acts, effort linked to interest, or fatigue to disinterest, etc. These affective states, like those associated with perception, stay linked for a long time to the isolated actions of the subject without precise delimitation between what is specific to him and what is attributable to the external world, i.e., to other sources of possible activity and causality. By contrast, when "objects" become detached more and more distinctly from the global and undifferentiated configuration of primitive actions and percepts and become objects conceived as external to the self and independent of it, the situation becomes completely transformed. On the one hand, in close correlation with the construction of the object, awareness of "self" begins to be affirmed by means of the internal pole of reality, as opposed to the external or objective pole. On the other hand, objects are conceived by analogy with this self as active, alive, and conscious. This is particularly so with those exceptionally unpredictable and interesting objects—people. The elementary feelings of joy and sadness, of success and failure, etc., are now experienced as a function of this objectification of things and of people, from which interpersonal feelings will develop. The affective "object choice" which psychoanalysis contrasts with narcissism is thus correlated with the intellectual construction of the object, just as narcissism is correlated with lack of differentiation between the external world and the self. This "object choice" is first of all vested in the person of the mother, then (both negatively and positively) of the father and other relatives. This is the beginning of the sympathies and antipathies that will develop to such an extent in the course of the ensuing period.

2. EARLY CHILDHOOD FROM TWO TO SEVEN YEARS

With the appearance of language, behavior is profoundly modified both affectively and intellectually. In addition to all the real or material actions the child learns to master during this period, as he did during the preceding period, he now becomes able, thanks to language, to reconstitute his past actions in the form of recapitulation and to anticipate his future actions through verbal representation. This has three consequences essential to mental development: (1) the possibility of verbal exchange with other persons, which heralds the onset of the socialization of action; (2) the internalization of words, i.e., the appearance of thought itself, supported by internal language and a system of signs; (3) last and most important, the internalization of action as such which from now on, rather than being purely perceptual and motor as it has been heretofore, can represent itself intuitively by means of pictures and "mental experiments." From the affective point of view a parallel series of transformations follows: development of interpersonal feelings (sympathies and antipathies, respect, etc.) and of internal affectivity organized in a more stable manner than heretofore.

We shall examine these three general modifications of behavior (socialization, thought, and intuition) successively and then consider their affective repercussions. In order to make these various new manifestations comprehensible we must insist upon their continuity with previous behavior. With the appearance of language, the young child must cope not only with the physical universe, as was the case earlier on, but also with two new and closely allied worlds: the social world and the world of inner representations. It should be recalled that with respect to material objects or bodies, the infant started with an egocentric attitude, in which the incorporation of objects into his own activity prevailed over accommodation (remodification of behavior as a result of experience). Thereafter, he gradually proceeds to situate himself in an objective universe (in which assimilation to the subject and accommodation to the real world become harmonized). Similarly, the young child at first reacts to social relations and to emergent thinking with unconscious egocentricity, which perpetuates the egocentricity of infancy. This egocentricity is then progressively given up, according to the laws of equilibration. These laws, however, are transposed to a higher level of functioning as a function of the need to cope with new realities. Throughout early childhood, therefore, one observes a partial repetition, on new behavioral planes, of the evolution already accomplished by the infant on the elementary plane of practical adaptations. These repetitions are highly instructive with respect to the intimate mechanisms of mental evolution.

A. The Socialization of Action

The most obvious result of the appearance of language is to permit verbal exchange and continuous communication among individuals. No doubt these interpersonal relations germinate as of the second half of the first year, thanks to imitation, since imitation is closely linked to sensorimotor development. There are no specific techniques of imitation. The infant learns to imitate gradually. At first, he copies gestures he can already execute spontaneously by watching the movements of the body and particularly the hands of other persons. As his capacity for sensorimotor imitation increases, he is able to copy the movements of others with increasing precision, provided these movements are within his repertoire of behavior. Ultimately, the child reproduces new, more complex movements. For example, it is more difficult for him to copy movements having to do with the parts of his body not visible to him, such as the face and the head. The imitation of sounds follows a similar course, and when sounds are associated with specific actions they result in the acquisition of language itself (elementary word-phrases, then substantives and differentiated verbs, and finally sentences as such). Until a definite form of language is acquired, interpersonal relations are limited to the imitation of corporal and other external gestures and to a global affective relationship without differentiated communication. With language, by contrast, the inner life itself can be communicated. In fact, thought becomes conscious to the degree to which the child is able to communicate it.

What are the elementary functions of language? It is instructive to record, at regular intervals for several hours at a stretch, all that is said by two to seven year old children.[5] These samples of language, which may be either spontaneous or elicited, can then be analyzed from the point of view of understanding the fundamental social relations of the child. Three broad categories of factors emerge:

First, there is the subordination and psychological constraint imposed by the adult on the child. With language the child discovers the unsuspected riches of a world of realities superior to himself. Prior to the acquisition of language, his parents and the adults who surround the child already appeared as big, strong beings, who engaged in unpredictable and often mysterious activities. Once the child attains language, however, these same beings reveal their thoughts and wishes. This new universe impinges upon him with its incomparable attractions of seduction and prestige. As Baldwin [1906] has pointed out, the child derives an "ego ideal" from his superiors, whom he seeks to emulate; and as Bovet [1928] has indicated, respect makes the child accept the orders and commands of the adult and makes him consider them obligatory. Beyond this particular kernel of obedience, the child develops an unconscious intellectual and affective submission as a result of the psychological constraint imposed by the adult.

Secondly, there are all the exchanges with the adult himself or with other children; these intercommunications also play a decisive role in determining the course of action. To the extent that they lead to the formulation of action itself and to the recall of past actions, they transform material behavior into thought. As Janet [1928] has pointed out, memory is linked to verbal recall, reflection to discussion, belief to engagement or to a promise, and thought to the entirety of internal or external language. One must, nonetheless, ask whether the child is completely aware of how to communicate his thoughts and is capable of taking the point of view of others or whether socialization has to be learned in order to achieve real cooperation. In this regard, the analysis of the functions of spontaneous language is instructive. The conversations among young children remain rudimentary and linked to material action itself. Until seven years of age children scarcely know how to have discussions among themselves and confine themselves to making contradictory affirmations. When they try to furnish explanations to others, they are not really able to put themselves in the place of the other person, who does not know what they are talking about; they speak as though they were talking to themselves. For example, while working in the same room or at the same table, each child speaks for himself, even though he thinks he is listening to and understands the others. This kind of "collective monologue" is really a mutual excitation to action rather than a real exchange of ideas. The same characteristics are found in children's collective games. In a game of marbles, for example, older children submit to certain rules and adjust their individual games to those of others, whereas young children play for themselves without bothering about the rules of their playmates.

There is a third category of observations. The small child speaks not only to others, he constantly talks to himself in various monologues that are an accompaniment to his games and actions. While these soliloquies are comparable to what will later be the continuous internal language of the adolescent or the adult, they are different in that they are spoken aloud and serve as an adjunct to immediate action. These true monologues, as well as collective monologues, constitute more than one-third of the spontaneous language of children from three to four years and diminish gradually up to the age of seven.

An examination of the spontaneous language of children and their behavior in collective games shows, therefore, that early social behavior remains midway along the road between egocentrism and true socialization. Rather than extricating himself from his own point of view in order to coordinate it with the viewpoints of others, the child still remains unconsciously centered on himself. This egocentricity vis-à-vis the social group reproduces and prolongs the egocentricity we have already noted in the infant vis-à-vis the physical universe. In both cases there is a lack of differentiation between the self and external reality, which at this stage is represented by other individuals and no longer simply by objects. In both cases this initial confusion results in the primacy of the child's own point of view. The psychological and, *a fortiori*, material constraint exercised by the adult on the child by no means precludes this egocentricity in the small child's relationship to the adult. While submitting to the adult and seeing him as highly superior to himself, the small child frequently reduces the adult to his own scale, just as certain naïve believers do with respect to divinity. This results in a compromise between his own point of view and that of the superior being, rather than in a well-differentiated coordination between the two.

B. The Genesis of Thought

As a function of general modifications of action and through the influence of language and socialization, intelligence is transformed during early childhood from simple sensorimotor or practical intelligence to thought itself. Language enables the subject to describe his actions. It allows him both to reconstitute the past (to evoke it in the absence of the objects which were previously acted upon) and to anticipate future, not yet executed, actions to the point where sometimes actions are replaced by words and are never actually performed. This is the point of departure for thought. At the same time, language leads to a socialization of actions which gives rise to acts of thought no longer exclusively related to the self that engenders them; from now on thought is related to a broader plane of communication. Language is, in effect, the vehicle for concepts and ideas that belong to everyone, and it reinforces individual thinking with a vast system of collective concepts. The child becomes immersed in these concepts as soon as he masters words.

Thought is like all behavior. The child does not adapt himself right away to the new realities he is discovering and gradually constructing for himself. He must start by laboriously incorporating them within himself and into his own activity. This egocentric assimilation characterizes the beginnings of thought just as it characterizes the process of socialization. At every stage during the period from two to seven years, one finds all the transitions between two extreme forms of thought, but the second form gradually gains precedence over the first. The first of these forms is thought by means of pure incorporation or assimilation, in which egocentricity excludes all objectivity. The second form is that of thought adapted to others and to reality,

which is a preparation for logical thought. Most infantile thinking oscillates between these two extremes.

Pure egocentric thought appears as a kind of game which
might be called "symbolic play." Practically every form of
psychological activity is initially enacted in play. At any rate,
play constitutes a functional exercise of these activities. Cognitive activity thus initiates play, and play in turn reinforces
cognitive activity. Well before the appearance of language, the
sensorimotor functions are used in pure exercise play in which
movements and percepts are activated without the intervention
of thought or of socialization. At the level of collective life
(seven to twelve years), by contrast, children participate in
games with rules which entail certain common obligations.
Between the two extremes there is a different form of play very
characteristic of young children. It employs thought, but
thought that is almost entirely idiosyncratic and has a minimum of collective elements. This is symbolic play or imaginative and imitative play. There are numerous examples: playing
with dolls, playing house, etc. It is easy to see that this symbolic
play constitutes a real activity of thought but remains essentially egocentric. Its function is to satisfy the self by transforming what is real into what is desired. The child who plays with
dolls remakes his own life as he would like it to be. He relives
all his pleasures, resolves all his conflicts. Above all, he compen-
sates for and completes reality by means of a fiction.

Symbolic play is not an attempt by the subject to submit to
reality but rather a deforming assimilation of reality to the self.
If language intervenes in this kind of imaginative thinking, it is
mostly through pictures or symbols. While the symbol is certainly a sign, like a word or verbal sign, it is a personal sign
elaborated by the individual without the help of others and
often understood only by the subject himself because the imagery refers to memories and states that have been experienced
intimately and personally. Symbolic play thus exemplifies egocentric thinking in an almost pure state and in this regard is
surpassed only by reverie and dreams.

At the other extreme there is the form of thought that is the most reality-oriented of any to be found in early childhood. This we have called intuitive thought. In a sense, it is sensori-motor experience and coordination that can be reconstituted or anticipated thanks to the ability to use representation. We shall return to this form of thought later (under subheading C) because intuition is in some measure the logic of early childhood.

Between these two extreme types of thought there is a form of purely verbal thought, serious by contrast with play, but more removed from reality than intuition itself. It is the everyday thinking common to children from two to seven years, and it is extremely interesting to note how it prolongs the mechanisms of assimilation and reality construction of the preverbal period.

In order to understand how the small child thinks spontaneously, there is no more instructive method than to inventory and analyze the many questions he poses almost as soon as he is able to talk.[6] Among these questions the most primitive are directed simply toward knowing "where" desired objects are and what less well-known objects are called: "What is it?" From the age of three (and sometimes much earlier) to the age of seven, a question that occurs with increasing frequency is the well-known "why" of young children, to which adults are sometimes at pains to find an answer. What is its general significance? The word "why" may have two distinct meanings for the adult: the goal ("Why are you taking this road?") or the cause ("Why are the bodies falling?").[7] For the small child, "why" appears to have an undifferentiated significance midway between goal and cause but always implying both at the same time. "Why is it rolling?" a child of six may ask, pointing to a marble rolling gently down toward a person at the base of a hill. He is told, "Because it's on an incline." This is a uniquely physical causal reply, and the child, not satisfied with this explanation, asks another question, "It knows you are down there?" The child certainly does not impute human consciousness to the marble, and even though there may be a certain childhood "animism," this should not be interpreted as anything so gross as anthropomorphism. Nonetheless, the mechanical explanation is not satisfying to the child because he sees movement as necessarily oriented toward some end, and, in consequence, as confusingly intentional and directed. Thus the child wants to know both the cause and the purpose of the marble's movement.

Moreover, what frequently makes these "whys" of childhood so obscure to adults and accounts for the difficulties we have in giving satisfactory replies to children's questions is that, for many questions dealing with phenomena or events, there is no "because," since the events are fortuitous. The same six-year-old boy whose reaction to movement has been mentioned is surprised that there are two Salèves [8] above Geneva while there is only one Matterhorn above Zermatt: "Why are there two Salèves?" Another day he asks: "Why doesn't the Lake of Geneva go as far as Berne?" Not knowing how to reply to these bizarre questions, we posed them to other children of the same age, asking them what they would have replied. The reply presented no difficulty for them: "There is a big Salève for big races and big people and a little Salève for small walks and for children, and if Lake Geneva does not go as far as Berne, it's because each town has its own lake." In other words, there is no chance in nature, and everything is "made for" man and children according to an established and wise plan with the human being at its center. Thus it is the *raison d'être* of things that is sought by the "why," i.e., a reason that is both causal and finalistic. It is because he believes that there must be a reason for everything that the child is troubled by fortuitous phenomena and poses questions about them.

In short, the analysis of how the child poses questions demonstrates the still egocentric character of his thought on this new plane of reality representation in opposition to the organization of the practical universe (at which level he is already freed from his egocentrism). Everything happens as if the practical schemas (of action) are transferred to this new plane and perpetuated not only with finalism as we have just seen but also in other respects.

Childhood animism is the tendency to conceive things as living and endowed with intentions.[9] At the beginning of this period of childhood, an object is alive to the extent that it exercises an activity useful to man: the lamp that burns, the furnace that heats, the moon that shines, etc. Later on, life is attributed only to what is mobile and still later only to bodies that appear to move of themselves, such as the stars and the wind. Consciousness is associated with life, not a consciousness identical to that of man, but the minimum knowledge and intention necessary for things to accomplish their actions and, above all, to be able to move and direct themselves toward their assigned goals. Thus the clouds know that they move because they bring rain and, above all, they bring night (night is a large black cloud that fills the sky when one is supposed to go to sleep).

Later, only spontaneous movement is endowed with consciousness. For example, clouds no longer know anything "because the wind pushes them." With respect to the wind, while it does not know anything as we do "because it is not a person"; nevertheless, "The wind knows it is blowing because it is the wind who is blowing!" Stellar bodies are particularly intelligent: the moon follows us on our walks and comes back behind us when we change paths. A deaf and dumb subject studied by W. James [10] even thought that the moon denounced him when he stole at night and pushed this reflection to the point of wondering whether the moon might have a relationship with his mother who had died shortly before. As for normal children, they are practically unanimous in believing that the moon accompanies them on a walk, and their egocentricity impedes them from thinking what the moon would do in the presence of people strolling in opposite directions. After seven years, by contrast, this question (i.e., When you are out for a walk what does the moon do? [Piaget, 1951 (c)]) suffices to lead them to the opinion that the movements of the moon are simply apparent when its disc follows us.

It is evident that such animism results from assimilation of things into one's own activity, as in the case of finalism already discussed. But just as the sensorimotor egocentricity of the infant results in a lack of differentiation between the self and the external world and not in a narcissistic hypertrophy of the awareness of self, so do animism and finalism express a confusion or a lack of differentiation between the internal or subjective world and the physical universe. In effect, the small child animates inert bodies and materializes the world of the mind. Thought for him is a voice, a voice that is in the mouth or "a little voice that is behind things," and this voice is "from the wind" (cf. the ancient terms "anima," "psyche," "rouach," etc.). Dreams are pictures, usually somewhat frightening, sent by nocturnal lights (the moon, street lamps) or the air itself, which come and fill the room. A little later, dreams are conceived as coming from ourselves, but they are pictures nonetheless, in the head when we are awake and sitting on the bed or in the room when we are asleep. When we see ourselves in a dream, then we have a double: we are in bed watching the dream but are also "in the dream," as a function of an immaterial double or image. For our part, we do not believe that the possible resemblances between the thought of the child and that of primitive man (we shall see, further on, some parallels with Greek physics) are due to any kind of heredity. The permanence of the laws of mental development suffice to explain these convergences, and since all men, including "primitive men," started by being children, childhood thinking preceded the thought of our most distant ancestors just as it does our own!

To finalism and animism one may add artificialism, or the belief that everything has been built by man or by a divine being who fabricates things in human fashion. The child finds no contradiction between artificialism and animism, since for him babies themselves are both manufactured and living. The entire universe is fabricated: mountains "grow" because stones have been manufactured and then planted; lakes have been hollowed out, and for a long time the child believes that cities are built before the lakes adjacent to them.

The whole sense of causality that develops during early childhood is characterized by the same lack of differentiation between the psychological and the physical and by intellectual egocentricity. Natural laws are confounded with moral laws and determinism with obligation. Boats float because they have to, and the moon shines only at night "because it is not the moon who decides." Movement is conceived as a transitive state tending toward a goal which terminates the movement. Springs flow because they have the momentum to go into lakes, but this momentum does not allow them to go up toward mountains. The idea of force gives rise to particularly curious statements. Force is active and substantial; it is linked to each body but is not transmissible. As is the case in Aristotle's physics, the movement of a body is explained by virtue of the combination of an external trigger and an internal force, both of which are necessary. For example, the clouds are pushed by the wind, but they also create wind themselves as they move forward. This explanation, which recalls the celebrated peripatetic schema of the movement of projectiles, is elaborated by the child himself. A ball does not fall to the ground right away when it is thrown because it is pushed by the air created by the displacement of the hand and by the air the ball itself sets in motion as it moves. Similarly, stream water is moved by the momentum it gains by its contact with the stones over which it passes, etc.

In summary, these diverse manifestations of this early thinking are consistent in their prelogical character. They all manifest a deforming assimilation of reality to the child's own activity. Physical movements are directed toward a goal because the child's own movements are goal-oriented. Force is active and substantial because it is conceived on the model of muscular strength. Physical reality is animated and alive, while natural laws must be obeyed. In short, all of reality is construed with the self as the model. Are these schemata of egocentric assimilation, which are widespread in symbolic play and still dominate verbal thought, capable of more precise accommodations under certain experimental conditions? This is what we shall see apropos of the development of intuitive mechanisms.

C. Intuition

One quality stands out in the thinking of the young child: he constantly makes assertions without trying to support them with facts. This lack of attempts at proof stems from the character of the child's social behavior at this age, i.e., from his egocentricity conceived as a lack of differentiation between his own point of view and that of others. It is only vis-à-vis others that we are led to seek evidence for our statements. We always believe ourselves without further ado until we learn to consider the objections of others and to internalize such discussions in the form of reflection. In questioning children under seven years one is struck by the poverty of their proofs, by their incapacity to find grounds for their statements, and even by the difficulty they experience in recapitulating through retrospection how they reached their conclusions. By the same token, the child from four to seven years does not know how to define the concepts he employs and confines himself to designating corresponding objects or to defining them by their usage ("It is for . . ."). He is influenced by finalism and by the difficulty he experiences in justifying the concepts he employs.

It can be maintained that the child of this age is unable to verbalize his thought and that his real domain is still that of action and manipulation. Undoubtedly this is true, but even in this domain is he in fact more "logical?" We shall make a distinction between intelligence that is properly "practical" and thought that tends toward experimentally-based knowledge.

There is a "practical intelligence" that plays a considerable role between the ages of two and seven years. On the one hand, it prolongs sensorimotor intelligence from the preverbal period, and on the other, it prepares for the technical ideas that will develop in adulthood. This developing practical intelligence has been studied by means of many ingenious devices (attaining objects through intermediary instruments of various kinds: sticks, hooks, pushers, etc.), and it has been shown that the child is frequently much more advanced in action than in language. But even in this practical area all kinds of primitive forms of active behavior reminiscent of prelogical thinking [11] at the same level have been observed [Rey, 1935].

Let us return to the thinking proper of this period of development and try to analyze it on an experimental rather than a verbal plane. How will the child behave when faced with the manipulation of specific materials, where each affirmation he makes can be verified by direct contact with the facts? Will he reason logically, or will the schemata of assimilation conserve part of their egocentricity while at the same time accommodating themselves as much as possible to the experiment in progress? Experimentation has shown decisively that until the age of seven the child remains prelogical. In place of logic he substitutes the mechanism of intuition—simple internalization of percepts and movements in the form of representational images and "mental experiences"—which prolongs the sensorimotor schemata without true rational coordination.

Let us start with a concrete example.[12] Present the subject with six or eight blue discs aligned with small spaces between them and ask him to pick out the same number of red discs from a pile at hand. At four to five years, on the average, children will construct an arrangement of red discs of exactly the same length as the blue discs but without bothering about the number of elements nor about making each red disc correspond to each blue one. Here we see an example of a primitive form of intuition which consists of evaluating quantity merely by the space it occupies, i.e., by the global perceptual qualities of the whole collection that is envisaged, without regard to its constituent relationships. Between five and six years, by contrast, there is a much more interesting reaction. The child matches a red disc with each blue one and concludes that the correspondence of each element results in the equality of the two series. However, if we move out the discs at the extreme ends of the red series so that they are no longer exactly underneath the blue ones but a little to one side, the child, who saw that nothing was added or subtracted, believes that the two series are no longer equivalent and contends that the longer series contains "more discs." If one of the series of discs is piled together in a heap and the other is left untouched, the apparent equivalence of the two series is undermined even further. Hence, there is equivalence as long as there is visual or optical correspondence, but the equality is not maintained by any logical means. In other words, this is not a rational operation; it is simply an intuition. This intuition is articulated rather than global, but it is nonetheless intuitive, i.e., subject to the primacy of perception.

What do such intuitions consist of? Two other instances will suffice as examples.[18] (1) Present the subject with three different colored balls—A, B, C—on a wire which is then passed through a tube. Children who see the balls start in the order A, B, C, expect to see them at the other end of the tube in the same order A, B, C. Their intuition is correct. But what if the tube is rotated 180° in the opposite direction before the balls reappear? The youngest children do not anticipate the order C, B, A and are completely surprised by the outcome. When they can predict the outcome by means of articulated intuition, the tube can be twice rotated so that in one direction the order comes out C, B, A, and in the other direction A, B, C. Not only do they not understand this, but, when they see first A and then C coming out at the head of the series, they expect next time to see the middle ball in the lead position! (2) When two different objects follow the same path and the same direction and the first object passes the second, at all ages the child concludes that the first object "is going faster." But if the first object goes by a longer route without catching up to the second or goes backward or when the two follow two concentric circles, the child does not understand the inequality of speed even if there are great differences between the two routes. The intuition of speed thus reduces to the perception of objects overtaking one another and does not include an understanding of the relationship between time and distance covered, as is true for older children and adults.

What are these elementary intuitions of spatial or optical relationships of the order A, B, C or of overtaking? They are simply perceptual or action schemata, i.e., sensorimotor schemata, transposed or internalized as representations. They are pictures or imitations of reality midway between actual experience and "mental experience." They are not as yet logical operations that can be generalized and combined one with the other.

What do these intuitions lack in order to become operational and to become transformed into a logical system? They lack the capacity to prolong actions already familiar to the subject so that they become both mobile and reversible. Primary intuitions are always characterized by rigidity and irreversibility. They are comparable to perceptual schemata and habits which unfold in a definite sequence that cannot be reversed. All habits in effect are irreversible. For example, one writes from left to right, and it would necessitate a whole new learning process in order to write from right to left (and vice versa for the Arabs). The same holds true for percepts, since they follow a unidirectional course of events, and for acts of sensorimotor intelligence which strive toward a goal but do not proceed backward (except in certain special cases). It is thus quite natural that a young child's thinking starts by being irreversible and especially that, when percepts and movements are internalized in the form of representations, they remain relatively immobile and irreversible. Primary intuition is no more than a sensorimotor schema transposed into an act of thought so that it naturally inherits the characteristics of the sensorimotor schema. Primary intuition is a positive acquisition and it would be sufficient to prolong internalized action in the direction of reversible mobility in order for the intuition to be transformed into an "operation."

Articulated intuition does in fact progress in this direction. Whereas primary intuition is only the representation of a global action, articulated intuition goes beyond it in the double sense that it can anticipate the consequences of action and reconstitute previous states. Articulated intuition is, however, still irreversible. For example, if an optical arrangement is changed, the child cannot mentally put the elements back in their original order. If the tube of balls is half turned, the reversed order escapes the subject, etc. However, the beginnings of anticipation and reconstitution prepare for reversibility. They constitute a regulation of the initial intuition and this regulation prepares for the operations. Articulated intuition is capable of attaining a more stable and mobile level of equilibrium than that of sensorimotor action alone. Thus, thinking at this stage shows great progress over preverbal intelligence. Compared to logic, intuition is in less stable equilibrium because of its lack of reversibility, but compared to preverbal acts it marks a definite advance in equilibrium.

D. The Affective Life

The transformations of action, by-products of the beginnings of socialization, not only affect intelligence and thought but also have profound repercussions on the affective life. As we have already seen at the preverbal period, there is a close parallel between the development of affectivity and that of the intellectual functions, since these are two indissociable aspects of every action. In all behavior the motives and energizing dynamisms reveal affectivity, while the techniques and adjustment of the means employed constitute the cognitive sensorimotor or rational aspect. There is never a purely intellectual action, and numerous emotions, interests, values, impressions of harmony, etc., intervene—for example, in the solving of a mathematical problem. Likewise, there is never a purely affective act, e.g., love presupposes comprehension. Always and everywhere, in object-related behavior as well as in interpersonal behavior, both elements are involved because the one presupposes the other. There are those who are more interested in people than things or abstractions and vice versa, which makes the former appear more sentimental and the latter more arid, but it is merely a question of different behavior and different emotions. Each necessarily employs both intelligence and affectivity.

At the level of development we are now considering, there are three new affective developments: the development of interpersonal emotions (affections, sympathies, and antipathies) linked to the socialization of action; the appearance of intuitive moral sentiments as a by-product of the relationships between adults and children; and the regulation of interests and values, linked to intuitive thought in general.

Let us start with the third aspect, since it is the most elementary. Interest is, in effect, the prolongation of needs. It represents the relationship between an object and a need, since an object is of interest to the extent that it fulfills a need. Interest is the proper orientation for every act of mental assimilation. Mental assimilation is the incorporation of an object into the activity of the subject, and this incorporative relationship between the object and the ego is none other than interest in the most immediate sense of the term ("inter-esse"). As such, interest commences with the beginnings of psychological life and plays an essential role in the development of sensorimotor intelligence. But with the development of intuitive thought, interests multiply and differentiate and give rise to a progressive dissociation between the energizing mechanisms that imply interest and the values interest engenders.

Interest appears in two complementary forms. On the one hand, it is a regulator of energy, as Claparède [1951] has shown. Its intervention mobilizes internal reserves of strength, and it suffices for work to be interesting in order for it to appear easy and for fatigue to diminish. It is for this reason, for example, that students make infinitely better progress when an appeal is made to their interests and proposed studies correspond to their needs. On the other hand, interest implies a system of values which, in the vernacular, constitute "interests" (in contrast to "interest") [14] that become differentiated in the course of mental development by assigning ever more complex goals to action. These values depend on another system of regulations which command internal energies without depending on them and which tend to assure or re-establish the equilibrium of the self in ceaselessly completing activity by the incorporation of new forces or new external elements. It is for this reason that during early childhood we note the interest in words, in drawings, in pictures, in rhythms, in certain physical exercises, etc. All these realities acquire value for the subject to the extent that they fulfill his needs. His needs in turn are dependent on his momentary mental equilibrium and above all on the new incorporations necessary to the maintenance of equilibrium.

Closely linked to the interests or activity-related values are the feelings of self-evaluation: the well-known "feelings of inferiority" or "feelings of superiority." All the successes and failures of the subject's own activity become registered in a kind of permanent scale of values, successes elevating his pretensions and failures lowering them with regard to his future actions.[15] As a result, the individual is gradually led to evaluate himself, a factor which may have great repercussions on his whole development. In particular, certain anxieties result from real, but more often imaginary, failures.

The system constituted by these numerous values exerts its greatest influence upon affective interpersonal relationships. Just as intuitive or representational thought is linked, thanks to language and the existence of verbal signs, to intellectual exchanges among individuals, so spontaneous feelings between one person and another grow from an increasingly rich exchange of values. As soon as communication is possible between the small child and the people about him, a subtle game of sympathies and antipathies develops, which elaborates and differentiates the elementary feelings already noted in the preceding stage of development. As a general rule, there is sympathy for persons who respond to the interests of the subject and who value him. Sympathy presupposes on the one hand a positive mutual evaluation and on the other hand a set of shared values. This is what language expresses by saying that people who like each other "get along together," "have the same tastes," etc. It is on the basis of these shared values that positive mutual evaluation takes place. Conversely, antipathy grows from devaluation and often proceeds from an absence of common tastes and shared values. It suffices to observe the small child in the choice of his first friends or in his reaction to adults who are strangers to the family in order to follow the development of these interpersonal evaluations.

As for the love of a child for his parents, blood ties could hardly explain the intimate communion of valuation which makes practically all the values of the small child dependent on the image of his mother and father. Among the interpersonal values that are constituted in this way, there are some which are of particular note, namely, those which the young child reserves for people he considers his superiors—certain older persons and his parents. A particular feeling is connected with these unilateral evaluations: respect. Respect consists of affection and fear, and fear is the reason for the inequality in such an affective relationship. As Bovet [1928] has shown, respect is the source of the first moral feelings. All that is needed is for the respected individuals to give orders and admonishments to the child for them to be felt as obligatory and thus to engender a feeling of duty.

The first moral precept of the child is obedience, and the first criterion of what is good is, for a long time, the will of the parents.[16] The moral values thus engendered are normative values in the sense that they are no longer determined by simple spontaneous regulations in the manner of sympathies or antipathies but rather, thanks to respect, by rules as such. Can we conclude then that in early childhood interpersonal feelings are capable of attaining the level of what we shall call affective operations (by comparison with logical operations), i.e., do systems of moral values rationally influence one another, as is the case in an autonomous moral conscience? It does not seem so, since the child's first moral feelings remain intuitive—as is the case with thought itself during this period of development. The morals of the young child remain essentially heteronomous, i.e., subject to an external will, which is that of the respected persons or parents. It is interesting in this respect to analyze the valuations of the child in a well-defined moral sphere, such as that of the lie.[17] Thanks to the mechanism of unilateral respect, the child accepts and recognizes the rule of behavior imposing veracity well before he himself understands the value of truth or the nature of lying. Through his habits of play and imagination and his spontaneous thinking (which affirms without proof and assimilates reality to his own activity without concern for true objectivity), the small child is led to modify reality and to bend it to his desires. He thus distorts the truth without misgivings and this is what we call the "pseudo lie" of small children (The Sterns' [1931] *"Scheinlüge"*). The child nonetheless accepts the rule of truthfulness and considers it right that he be blamed or punished for his own "lies." But how does he evaluate his "lies?" At first, the young child thinks there is nothing "bad" about lying as long as he is addressing peers. Only lies to adults are blameworthy, since it is adults who prohibit lies. Later he feels that the further the falsehood is from reality, the worse the lie, regardless of his intentions. One can, for example, ask a child to compare two lies: telling his mother that he has received a good grade at school when he has not been graded at all or telling her that he has been frightened by a dog as big as a cow. The small child understands only too well that the first of these lies is intended to obtain an unwarranted reward while the second is a simple exaggeration. Nonetheless, the first seems "less bad" because one does sometimes get good grades and, above all, because the statement is sufficiently plausible for the mother herself to be deceived! The second "lie" is worse and merits worse chastisement because "a

dog never is as big as all that." These reactions, which seem
fairly typical (they have recently been confirmed in a study
conducted at the University of Louvain), are most instructive.
They show how much the first moral values are derived from
unilateral respect and how these values are interpreted according to their formulation rather than their intent. In order for
these same values to be organized in a coherent and general
system, moral feelings must attain a certain autonomy, and for
this to occur respect must cease to be unilateral and become
mutual. It is particularly when this feeling develops between
friends or equals that lying to a friend becomes "just as bad as"
or worse than lying to an adult.

In short, interests, self-evaluations, spontaneous interpersonal
values, and intuitive moral values appear to constitute the
principal crystallization of the affective life at this level of
development.

3. CHILDHOOD FROM SEVEN TO TWELVE YEARS

The age of seven years, which coincides with the real start of
formal education, marks a decisive turning point in mental
development. In each of the complex areas of psychological life,
whether it be intelligence, affectivity, social relations, or individual activity, new forms of organization appear. These new
forms of organization assure the completion and more stabilized equilibrium of constructions already outlined in the preceding period and inaugurate an uninterrupted series of new
constructions.

Through this labyrinth we shall follow the same route as in
the previous section. We shall start with global action—both
social and individual—and first analyze the intellectual and
then the affective aspects of development during this period.

A. *The Progress and Socialization of Behavior*

In an activity-oriented school, where the children are at lib-
erty to work either in groups or alone and to talk while working,

one is struck by the difference between these children and classes of younger children. Among the younger children, there is no distinct dividing line between individual activity and collaboration. The young children talk, but one does not know whether they listen. Several of them may be at work on the same project, but one does not know if they are really helping one another. Among the older children, there is progress in two directions: individual concentration when the subject is working by himself and effective collaboration in the group. These two aspects of the behavior that starts at around seven years are in reality complementary and derive from the same sources. They are, in fact, so intimately linked that one is hard put to say whether the child has become capable of a certain degree of reflection because he has learned to cooperate with others or vice versa.

At about the age of seven the child becomes capable of cooperation because he no longer confuses his own point of view with that of others. He is able both to dissociate his point of view from that of others and to coordinate these different points of view. This is apparent from conversations among children. True discussions are now possible in that the children show comprehension with respect to the other's point of view and a search for justification or proof with respect to their own statements. Explanations between children develop on the plane of thought and not just on the level of material action. "Egocentric" language disappears almost entirely, and the grammatical structure of the child's spontaneous statements attests to his need for a connection between ideas and logical justification.

In the collective behavior of children there is a noticeable change in social attitudes after the age of seven, as can be seen in games involving rules. A collective game, such as marbles, presupposes numerous rules, defining the manner of shooting the marbles, placing them, the order of successive shots, the rights of appropriation in the event of success, etc. This is a game which, at least in our country, remains exclusively within the province of childhood and is not played beyond primary school. The game of marbles involves a whole body of rules and the jurisprudence its application requires constitutes an institution peculiar to children. This institution is nevertheless transmitted from generation to generation with a surprising strength of conservation. Now in early childhood, players of four to six years try to imitate the example of their elders and try to observe certain rules. But each child knows only a few of the rules and during the game does not bother about the rules of his neighbor if he is of the same age; each one plays in his own uncoordinated fashion. When young children are asked at the end of a game who has won, they are extremely surprised at the question, because from their point of view everyone wins. At this age, to win means to have had a good time. By contrast, the players of seven or more have progressed in two ways. Without yet knowing all the rules of the game by heart, they at least agree on the rules permitted during a particular game and control each other in such a way as to maintain equality before a single law. In addition, "to win" takes on a collective meaning. It is to succeed after a regulated competition, and it is clear that the recognition of the victory of one player over the others, as well as the gain in marbles which results from winning, presupposes well-regulated and conclusive discussions.

Closely connected with this progress of social behavior, there are transformations of individual action which appear to be both the causes and the effects of this progress. The essence of these transformations is that the child becomes capable of at least rudimentary reflection. Instead of the impulsive behavior of the small child, accompanied by unquestioned beliefs and intellectual egocentricity, the child of seven or eight thinks before acting and thus begins to conquer the difficult process of reflection. Reflection is nothing other than internal deliberation, that is to say, a discussion which is conducted with oneself just as it might be conducted with real interlocutors or opponents.[18] One could then say that reflection is internalized social discussion (just as thought itself presupposes internalized language). This view is in accordance with the general rule that one always ends by applying to oneself behavior acquired from others. Contrariwise, socialized discussion might also be described as externalized reflection. Since all human conduct is both social and individual, this problem, like all analogous questions, comes back to whether the chicken appears before the egg or the egg before the chicken.

The important point is that, in both respects, the child of seven years begins to be liberated from his social and intellectual egocentricity and becomes capable of new coordinations which will be of the utmost importance in the development of intelligence and affectivity. With respect to intelligence, we are now dealing with the beginnings of the construction of logic itself. Logic constitutes the system of relationships which permit the coordination of points of view corresponding to different individuals, as well as those which correspond to the successive percepts or intuitions of the same individual. With respect to affectivity, the same system of social and individual coordination engenders a morality of cooperation and personal autonomy in contrast to the intuitive heteronomous morality of the small child. This new system of values represents, in the affective sphere, the equivalent of logic in the realm of intelligence. The mental instruments which will facilitate logical and moral coordination are the operation in the field of intelligence and the will in the field of affectivity. Here we have two new realities, and as we shall see, they are closely related since both result from the same inversion or conversion of primitive egocentricity.

B. The Progress of Thought

When the egocentric forms of causality and representations of the world—i.e., those based on the child's own activity—start to decline under the influence of the factors just cited, new kinds of explication arise which derive from the preceding explications but also correct them. It is striking to note that among the first to appear are those which resemble certain theories advanced by the Greeks at the time of the decline of the mythological explications.

One of the simplest forms of rational relation between cause and effect is explication by means of identification. During the preceding age period thought was characterized by a mixture of animism and artificialism. With respect to the origin of the stars (a bizarre question to pose to children, but one which they frequently raise spontaneously) primitive types of causality are evident: for example, "The sun is born because we are born," and "It has grown because we have grown." When this gross egocentricity is on the decline, the child, while maintaining the idea of the growth of the stars, does not consider that they are derived by human or anthropomorphic means but through other natural bodies whose formation appears, at first glance, to be more readily understandable. Thus the sun and moon have come out from the clouds; little pieces of clouds have grown and "little moons" frequently grow in front of our eyes! But clouds themselves have come out of smoke or air. Stones are formed from the earth, the earth from water, etc. When things are no longer seen as growing like living beings, their derivation is no longer traced by the child to biological processes but to transmutations. It is easy to see the connection between these explications and the reduction of matter theories which were in vogue in the school of Miletus [19] (the "nature" or "physis" of things was a kind of growth for these philosophers and their "hylozoism" was closely related to the animism of the child).

Now what do these early types of explication consist of? Does childhood animism give way directly to a kind of causality based on the principle of identity? Does this well-known logical principle govern reason right away in the manner that certain philosophers [20] would have us believe? Certainly there is proof in these developments that egocentric assimilation and the principles of animism, finalism, and artificialism are in the process of becoming transformed into rational assimilation, i.e., into a structuring of reality by reason itself, but this rational assimilation is much more complex than pure and simple identification.

If, instead of attempting to follow children in their questions about distant realities such as the stars, the mountains, and the ocean, which can be dealt with only on the verbal plane, one questions them about tangible and plausible things, one is in for a great surprise. By the age of seven years, the child is capable of building explanations which are properly atomistic; this occurs at the period when he starts to count. To continue with our comparison, recall that the Greeks invented atomism soon after having speculated on the transmutation of substances, and note in particular that the first of the atomists was probably Pythagoras, who believed that the composition of bodies was based on material numbers or discontinuous points of substance. Of course, with rare exceptions (and there are some), the child does not generalize and differs from the Greek philosophers in that he does not construct a system. But when experience permits, he does have recourse to an explicit and quite rational atomism.

The simplest experiment in this regard consists of presenting the child with two glasses of water of the same shape and size, filled three-quarters full.[21] Two lumps of sugar are immersed in one glass, and the child is asked in advance if the water will rise. Once the sugar is immersed, the new water level is measured and the glass is weighed, so as to show that the glass containing the sugar weighs more than the other glass. While the sugar is dissolving, the following questions are asked:

1) Once the sugar is dissolved, will anything remain in the water?

2) Will the weight remain greater or become the same as the glass containing the clear water?

3) Will the level of the sugar water descend so as to become equal to the water level in the other glass or will it remain the way it is?

The child is asked to give reasons for all his replies. After the sugar has completely dissolved, the fact that the weight and volume (level) of the sugar water remain unchanged is pointed out and the discussion continues. The reactions observed at successive ages are so clear and regular that they can be used as a diagnostic procedure in the study of mental retardation (Inhelder, 1963). To begin with, the child of less than seven years generally denies the conservation of any of the dissolved sugar and *a fortiori* that of the weight and volume associated with it. For him the fact that the sugar dissolves implies that it is entirely annihilated and no longer has any reality. It is true that the taste of the sugar water remains, but according to the very young child the taste, too, is destined for annihilation in a few hours or days in the same way that a smell or a shadow disappears. At about the age of seven, by contrast, the child understands that the dissolved sugar remains in the water, i.e., there is conservation of the substance. But in what form? For some subjects, it becomes transformed into water or liquefied into a syrup which mixes with the water; an explanation by transmutation. In the case of the more advanced child, something else is proposed. The child states that he can see the piece of sugar frittering into "little crumbs" in the course of dissolving. Once it is realized that these "little bits" become constantly smaller, it is easy to understand that the water still contains invisible "little balls." And, these subjects add: "That is what makes the sweet taste." Thus atomism is born in the guise of a "metaphysics of dust" or powder, as a French philosopher has so wittily said. But it is still a qualitative atomism, since these "little balls" have neither weight nor volume and the child expects the weight to disappear and the level of the water to descend after the sugar has dissolved. At a later stage, which occurs at about nine years, the child reasons in the same way with respect to the substance but adds an essential element. Each small ball has its own weight, and if all the partial weights are added one will arrive at the weight of all the immersed sugar. By contrast, while he is capable of such a subtle *a priori* explanation for the conservation of weight, he is unable to do the same for volume and expects the level of the water to go down after the sugar has dissolved. Finally, at eleven to twelve years, the child generalizes his explanatory schema to the volume itself and declares that, since each little ball occupies its own small place, the sum of these spaces will equal the space taken up by the immersed sugar so that the level of the water will not go down.

Such is childhood atomism. This example is not unique. One obtains the same explanation in reverse when a grain of pop-corn is heated. For the young child the substance increases; at seven the substance is conserved without increasing—it merely swells and the weight changes; at nine to ten years the weight remains the same but not the volume; and toward twelve years, since flour is composed of invisible grains with a constant volume, these grains of powder simply move away from each other, separated by the hot air.

This atomism is remarkable not so much because of the representation of the granules, suggested by experience with powder or flour, but because of the deductive process it reveals. The whole is explained by the composition of its parts. This presupposes real operations of segmentation or partition and, inversely, of reunion or addition, as well as displacement by concentration or spreading out (like the pre-Socratics). Above all, it presupposes real principles of conservation, indicating that the operations at work are grouped into closed and coherent systems, in which the conservations represent "invariants."

We have just seen an early manifestation of the concept of permanence. It becomes associated successively with substance, weight, and volume. This is easy to demonstrate in other experiments. For example, the child is given two small balls of modeling clay of the same size and weight. One of the balls is then shaped into a flat cake, a sausage, or cut into pieces. Before the age of seven, the child believes that the quantity of matter, the weight, and the volume have changed. At seven to eight years, he sees the constancy of matter but still believes in the variability of the other qualities. Toward nine years, he recognizes the conservation of weight but not of volume, and at eleven to twelve years he recognizes the constancy of the volume. It is easy to demonstrate that, as of seven years, many other principles of conservation are also acquired. These conservations reflect the development of thinking and are completely absent in the younger child. It is only after the age of seven that one finds the conservation of lengths, surfaces, discontinuous wholes, etc. These ideas of invariance are equivalent, on the conceptual level, to what we have already seen in the sensorimotor schema of the "object," the practical invariant of action.

How are these concepts of conservation, which so profoundly differentiate the thought of the second period of childhood from the early years, elaborated? Exactly like atomism itself or, to speak more generally, like the causal explication based on partitive composition. These conservation concepts result from the interplay of operations coordinated among themselves into integrated systems whose most remarkable property, as compared with the intuitive thinking of the young child, is that of being reversible. The real reason children of this age recognize the conservation of substance or weight is not identity (the small child is just as capable of seeing that "nothing has been added or taken away" as is the older child), but the possibility of a rigorous return to the point of departure. The flat cake weighs as much as the ball, says the older child, because you can remake a ball from the cake. Later on we shall see the real significance of these operations. It is operations that result in a correction of perceptual intuition—which is always a victim of illusions of the moment—and which "decenter" egocentricity so as to transform transitory relationships into a coherent system of objective, permanent relations.

Before we continue, let us point out again the great advances achieved at this level of thinking. In addition to causality and concepts of conservation there is the mastery of time, rate, and space, concepts which are now general schemata of thought, rather than schemata of action or intuition.

The development of time concepts in children raises curious problems in connection with questions posed by contemporary science. At every age, of course, the child will be able to say of a moving object that goes from A to B to C that it was at A "before" being at B or at C and that it takes "more time" to go from A to C than from A to B. This is more or less the extent of the young child's temporal intuitions. If he is asked to compare two moving objects following parallel courses at different rates, it is apparent that: (1) the young child does not have the intuition of the simultaneity of terminal points, because he does not understand the existence of a time *common* to the two movements; (2) he does not have the intuition of the equality of two synchronous durations; (3) he does not understand the connection between duration and succession. For example, if boy X is younger than boy Y, the young child does not conclude that the second boy must necessarily have been born "after" the other. How, then, does he construct time? By the coordination of operations analogous to those which have already been discussed: placing events in successive order on the one hand and nesting the durations conceived as intervals between these events. The two systems are coherent because they fit together.

As for speed, young children of all ages correctly intuit that a moving object that passes another object is going faster than the second object. But if this passing is made invisible (by hiding the moving objects in tunnels of unequal length or by making the routes unequal but concentric circles) the intuition of speed fails. The rational concept of speed, on the other hand, conceived as a relationship between time and distance traveled evolves together with the time concept at around eight years of age.

There remains the construction of the space concept, which has immense importance both for the comprehension of the laws of development and for its pedagogical implications. Unfortunately, while we more or less understand the development of this concept in the form of a practical schema during the first two years, research with respect to the spontaneous geometry of the older child is far from being as advanced as the preceding concepts. All that we can say is that the fundamental ideas of order, continuity, distance, length, measurement, etc., only give rise in early childhood to extremely limited and distorted intuitions. Primitive space is neither homogeneous nor isotropic, nor continuous, etc.; above all, it is centered on the subject's standpoint rather than representing various points of view. It is again at approximately seven years of age that rational space is constructed by means of the same general operations whose formation we shall now discuss.

C. The Rational Operations

Intuition is the highest form of equilibrium attained by the thinking of young children and, in this sense, corresponds to the concrete operational thinking of middle childhood. The concrete operational kernel of intelligence merits detailed examination since it furnishes the key to an essential part of mental development.

It should be noted first that, while the concept of operation is well defined, it applies to many diverse realities. There are logical operations which underlie a system of class concepts and relations; arithmetic operations (addition, multiplication, etc., and their inverses); geometric operations (sections, displacements, etc.); temporal operations (seriation of events, i.e., the successive ordering of events and the nesting of intervals between them); mechanical operations; physical operations; etc. Psychologically, an operation is, above all, some kind of action (the act of combining individuals or numeric units, displacing them, etc.), whose origin is always perceptual, intuitive (representational), or motoric. The actions which are the starting point for operations are thus rooted in the sensorimotor schemata, i.e., in actual or mental (intuitive) experience. Before becoming operational, they constitute the substance of sensorimotor intelligence, then of intuition.

How can we explain the transition from intuitions to operations? Intuitions become transformed into operations as soon as they constitute groupings which are both composable and reversible. In other words, actions become operational when two actions of the same kind can be composed into a third action of the same kind and when these various actions can be compensated or annulled. Thus the action of combining (logical or arithmetic addition) is an operation, because several successive combinations are equivalent to a single combination (composition of additions) and because the combinations can be annulled by dissociations (subtractions).

It is remarkable to see the formation of a whole series of these groupings by children at about age seven. They transform the intuitions into operations of all kinds and explain the transformation of thinking described earlier. Above all, it is striking to see how these groupings are formed, often very rapidly, through a sort of total reorganization. No operation exists in an isolated state; it is always formed as a function of the totality of operations of the same kind. For example, a logical concept of class (combination of individuals) is not constructed in an isolated state but necessarily within a classification of the grouping of which it forms a part. A logical family relation (brother, uncle, etc.) is constituted only as a function of a set of analogous relations whose totality constitutes a system of relationships. Numbers do not appear independently of each other (3, 10, 2, 5, etc.); they are grasped only as elements within an ordered series: 1, 2, 3 . . . , etc. Likewise, values exist only as a function of a total system or "scale of values." An asymmetric relationship such as $B < C$ is intelligible only in relation to the possible seriation of the set: $O < A < B < C < D$ . . . etc. What is even more remarkable is that these systems of sets are formed only in the child's thinking in connection with the precise reversibility of the operations, so that they acquire a definite and complete structure right away.

A particularly clear example [22] of this is that of the qualitative seriation: $A < B < C$ . . . etc. During early childhood, a youngster can distinguish two sticks by their length and can judge that B is larger than A, but at this age level it is merely a conceptual or intuitive relationship and not a logical operation. If the young child is first shown sticks $A < B$, and then sticks $B < C$ while A is hidden under the table, and he is asked if A (which has just been compared with B) is larger or smaller than C (which is on the table with B), the child refuses to make a decision and asks to see the two together because he cannot deduce $A < C$ from $A < B$ and $B < C$. This occurs, naturally, only when the differences are not so great as to remain in the memory as picture images. When will the child be able to make this deduction? Not until he can construct a series or scale of sticks on the table, and, curiously enough, he will not be able to do so before six or seven years of age. To be sure, even a young child can order sticks of very different lengths, but this is simply a matter of constructing a staircase, i.e., a perceptual figure. By contrast, if the differences are small and he has to compare the elements of each pair of sticks in order to organize them, he will start by simply arranging them in pairs: CE; AC; BD; etc., without coordinating the pairs one with the other. Later he will make little series of three or four elements but still without coordinating the several part series. Subsequently, he will succeed with the whole series but only by trial and error and without knowing how to intersperse distinct new elements once the initial series has been completely arranged. Finally, at around the age of six and a half or seven, he discovers an operational method which consists of looking first for the smallest element, then for the smallest of those that remain, etc. He thus succeeds in constructing the whole series without trial and error and is also able to intersperse new elements. He then becomes capable of reasoning: $A < B$ and $B < C$, therefore $A < C$. It is also immediately apparent that this construction presupposes the inverse operation (operational reversibility). Each element is conceived both as smaller than all the following elements (relation $<$) and as larger than all the preceding elements (relation >). This allows the subject to discover a method of construction as well as to intersperse new elements after the total initial series has been constructed.

It is very interesting to note that, while the operations of seriation (coordination of asymmetric relation) are discovered at about the age of seven with respect to length or size, it is not until about the age of nine that the child can serially order weights in an analogous fashion (for example, the seriation of balls of the same size but different weight). It is not until eleven or twelve years that he acquires the same capacity with respect to volume (tested by means of immersing objects in water). By the same token, not until he is nine does the child conclude that $A < C$, if $A < B$ and $B < C$ with regard to weight, and not until he is eleven or twelve does he draw the same conclusions with respect to volume. It is evident that these operations are closely connected with the actual construction of the concepts of weight and volume and notably with the elaboration of the principles of conservation related to them (see above).

A second example of a total system of operations is the coordination of symmetrical relations,[28] in particular the relation among equalities: $A = B$; $B = C$; therefore $A = C$. Once again these groupings are linked to the construction of concepts themselves. These equality groupings appear as of the age of seven with respect to simple lengths and quantities, but not until the age of nine with respect to equalities of weight, while equalities with respect to volume do not appear until age twelve. Here is an example illustrating the equality of weights. The child is given some bars $A = B = C$ . . . of the same shape, size, and weight; then he is given pieces of lead, stone, etc., of different shapes but with the same weight as the bars. The child compares the lead with bar A and, to his astonishment, notes that the two weights are equal on the scale. He also sees that bar A's weight is equal to that of bar B. He is then asked whether bar B will weigh as much as the piece of lead.

Up until the age of eight and a half or nine years, he refuses to concede the equality. Not until the age at which all weight relations are coordinated will he be capable of this reversible composition.

A particularly apt example of the composition of symmetrical relations is that of "brother." [24] A small child of four or five years (let us call him Paul) has a brother, Etienne. When Paul is asked if his brother Etienne has a brother, he will frequently reply in the negative. The reason given is usually the following: "There are only two of us in the family and Etienne does not have a brother." Here we see clearly the the intellectual egocentricity that characterizes intuitive thought. Not knowing how to get away from his own point of view so as to see himself from another person's point of view, the child begins by denying the symmetry of the relationship of brother to brother because of a lack of reciprocity (i.e., symmetrical reversibility). By the same token, one can see how the logical or operational coordination of this kind of relationship is connected with an individual's social coordination and with the coordination of the intuitive points of view he has experienced.

We come now to the system of logical operations essential to the genesis of general concepts or "classes," hence of all classification.[25] The principle is simply the nesting of the parts in the whole or, conversely, the separation of the parts with respect to the whole. Here again, one must not confuse the intuitive totalities or simple collections of objects with the operational totalities or classes which are truly logical.

An easily reproducible experiment demonstrates that operational classes are constructed much later than one might think and shows how they are linked to reversible thinking. An open box containing about twenty brown wooden beads and two to three white wooden beads is presented to the subject. After he has manipulated the beads he is asked whether there are more wooden beads or more brown beads in the box. The great majority of children below seven years can only say, "There are more brown ones." This is so because, to the extent that they dissociate the whole ("all of wood") into two parts ("white" and "brown"), they are unable to compare one of these parts with the whole, which they have mentally destroyed; they can compare only the two parts. By contrast, at about seven years this difficulty attenuates and the whole can be compared to one of its parts, each part from then on being conceived as a true part of the whole (a part equals the whole minus the other parts, by virtue of the inverse operation).

Finally we come to the question of how numbers and arithmetic operations are constructed. We know that only the first numbers are accessible to the young child because these are intuitive numbers which correspond to perceptible figures. The indefinite series of numbers and, above all, the operations of addition (plus its inverse, subtraction) and multiplication (plus its inverse, division) are, on the average, accessible only after the age of seven. The reason for this is simple enough. Number is in reality a composite of some of the preceding operations and consequently presupposes their prior construction. A whole number is in effect a collection of equal units, a class whose subclasses are rendered equivalent by the suppression of their qualities. At the same time, it is an ordered series, a seriation of the relations of order. Its dual cardinal and ordinal nature thus results from a fusion of the logical systems of nesting and seriation, which explains why true number concepts appear at the same time as the qualitative operations. It is readily understandable, therefore, that the term-by-term correspondences which we have analyzed above (II C) remain intuitive during early childhood. They do not become operational and do not constitute numerical operations until the child reaches the point where he is able to coordinate the operations of seriation and nesting of parts in wholes (classes). It is only at this point that term-by-term correspondence brings with it the enduring equivalence of corresponding collections and thus engenders true number.[26]

We may draw a general conclusion: a child's thinking becomes logical only through the organization of systems of operations which obey the laws common to all groupings: (1) Composition: two operations may combine to give another operation of the grouping (e.g., +1 +1 = +2). (2) Reversibility: every operation can be inverted (e.g., +1 becomes inverted to −1). (3) The direct operation and its inverse gives rise to an identical or null operation (e.g., +1 −1 = 0). (4) Operations can combine with one another in all kinds of ways. This general structure, which mathematicians call "groups," characterizes all the systems of operations already described except that in the logical or qualitative domains (seriation of relations, nesting of classes, etc.), conditions (3) and (4) present certain peculiarities as a result of the fact that a class or relation added to itself does not change. In this case, we speak of a "grouping," which is an even more elementary and general concept than group.

The passage from intuition to logic or to mathematical operations is effectuated during the course of middle childhood by the construction of groupings and groups. Concepts and relations cannot be constructed in isolation but from the outset constitute organized sets in which all the elements are interdependent and in equilibrium. This structure, proper to mental assimilation of an operational order, assures the mind of an equilibrium considerably superior to that of intuitive or egocentric assimilation. The attained reversibility is a manifestation of a permanent equilibrium between the assimilation of things to the mind and the accommodation of the mind to things. Thus, when the mind goes beyond its immediate point of view in order to "group" relations, it attains a state of coherence and noncontradiction paralleled by cooperation on the social plane (see A). In both cases the self is subordinated to the laws of reciprocity.

D. Affectivity, Will, and Moral Feelings

These foregoing remarks attest to the profound transformations that occur in affectivity during middle childhood. Cooperation among individuals coordinates their points of view into a reciprocity which assures both the autonomy of the individual and the cohesion of the group. Similarly, the grouping of intellectual operations places diverse intuitive points of view in a reversible set that is free of contradictions. Thus, affectivity from seven to twelve years is characterized by the appearance of new moral feelings and, above all, by an organization of will, which culminates in a better integration of the self and a more effective regulation of affective life.

We have already seen (II D) how the first moral feelings ensue from the unilateral respect of the young child for his parents or other adults and how this respect leads to the formation of a morality of obedience or heteronomy. A new feeling, which arises as a function of cooperation among children and which social life engenders, consists essentially of mutual respect. There is mutual respect when two individuals attribute to each other equivalent personal value and do not confine themselves to evaluating each other's specific actions. Genetically, mutual respect stems from unilateral respect. Frequently an individual feels that another person is superior in some respect while there is reciprocity in other respects. If this is the case, a mutual global valuation follows sooner or later. In general, there is mutual respect in all friendships based on esteem, in all collaborations which exclude authority, etc.

Mutual respect leads to new forms of moral feeling distinct from initial external obedience. In the first place, let us mention the transformation of feelings concerning rules, rules linking children to one another as well as those linking the child and the adult.

Recall, for example, the manner in which children submit to the rules of a collective game even when it is a game peculiar to children, such as a game of marbles. Whereas young children play any which way, each according to isolated rules borrowed from his elders, boys over the age of seven submit in a much more precise and coordinated fashion to a set of common rules. How do they see these rules and how do they feel about them? This question can be answered by asking each individual player to invent a new rule, not based on those handed down to him. He is then asked to say whether or not his innovation would constitute a "true rule" once it had spread through imitation by the younger children. Curiously enough there is a great difference in reaction between the younger and older children. While in practice the younger children, who are dominated by the unilateral respect they feel for their elders, play without much concern for obedience to recognized rules, in general they refuse to concede that the new rule could ever be a "true rule." According to them, the only true rules are those that have always been used, those which were followed by the son of William Tell or by the children of Adam and Eve. No rule invented now by a child, even if it should spread to future generations, is really "true." Moreover, "true rules," eternal rules, do not emanate from children. It is the "gentlemen of the government," the "leading men," or God himself who has imposed the rules. One sees how far respect for the rules transmitted by elders can go. The reaction of the older children is quite different. The new rule can become "true" if each child adopts it; a true rule is merely the expression of a mutual agreement. The older child says that all rules of the game are rooted in a sort of contract among the players. Here we see mutual respect at work. The rule is no longer respected as the product of an external will but as the result of an explicit or tacit accord. For this reason the rule is truly respected in practice and not just in its verbal formulations. It is obligatory to the extent that the individual consents autonomously to the agreement on which the rule is based. That is why mutual respect entails a whole series of moral feelings unknown beforehand: honesty among players, which prohibits cheating—not just because cheating is "forbidden," but because it violates agreement among individuals who esteem one another; camaraderie; fair play; etc. It is only at this age that the child starts to comprehend the implications of lying, and it is understandable from the foregoing that deceit among friends is considered more serious than lying to adults.

A particularly remarkable affective product of mutual respect is the feeling of justice, a feeling that is very strong among friends and affects the relationships between children and adults to the point where relationships with parents may be changed. For young children obedience is primary: the concept of what is just is confused with what is demanded or imposed from on high. It is particularly striking, when young children are questioned about stories they have been told about lying, etc., to see how severe they are in their ideas of punishment. In their verbal judgments, if not in practice, they always find the severest punishment just. They make no distinction among sanctions as a function of intent but only with regard to the actual acts themselves (i.e., "objective" responsibility, as in the case of primitive peoples). By contrast, older children hold strongly to the conviction of a distributive justice based on strict equality and a retributive justice which pertains to intentions and circumstances rather than to the actions themselves. Where does this feeling of justice come from? Awareness of what is just and unjust ordinarily appears as a reaction to the adult rather than an acquisition from him. Through some unintentional or imaginary injustice of which the child is a victim, he starts to dissociate justice and submission. From then on, it is essentially cooperation and mutual respect among children that develop feelings of justice. Again, in collective games it is easy to point out numerous facts related to feelings of equality and distributive justice among friends of the same age. Without doubt these are among the most powerful moral feelings of the child.

The mutual respect that gradually becomes differentiated from unilateral respect leads to a new organization of moral values. Its principal characteristic is that it imputes relative autonomy to the moral conscience of individuals. From this point of view the moral of cooperation can be considered as a higher form of equilibrium than the moral of simple submission. With respect to the latter, we have spoken about "intuitive" moral feelings. The organization of moral values that characterizes middle childhood is, by contrast, comparable to logic itself; it is the logic of values or of action among individuals, just as logic is a kind of moral for thought. Honesty, a sense of justice, and reciprocity together form a rational system of personal values. Without exaggeration this system can be compared to the "groupings" of relations or concepts that characterize logic, the only difference being that here values are grouped according to a scale rather than by objective relationships.

If morality in the form of the coordination of values is comparable to a logical "grouping," then it is also true that interpersonal feelings give rise to a kind of operation. At first glance, it seems that the affective life is purely intuitive and that its spontaneity excludes anything approaching an intellectual operation. In reality this romantic notion is true only of early childhood, when impulsivity precludes all directedness of thought as well as of the emotions. By contrast, to the extent that the emotions become organized, they emerge as regulations whose final form of equilibrium is none other than the will. Thus, will is the true affective equivalent of the operation in reason. Will is a late-appearing function. The real exercise of will is linked to the functioning of the autonomous moral feelings, which is why we have waited until this stage to discuss it.

Will is frequently confused with quite different mechanisms, and for this reason many writers state that it is formed at the elementary stages of development. It is frequently reduced to a simple manifestation of the energy the subject has at his disposal. For example, the young child who always perseveres until he attains his goal is said to have will power. This is said particularly when he exerts his energy to do the opposite of what is wanted of him, as may be the case in the period of independence and contrariness often seen between the ages of three and four (the well-known "Trotzalter"). Will, however, is by no means energy itself at the service of certain tendencies. It is a regulator of energy, which is something quite different, a regulator that favors certain tendencies at the expense of others. Will is also frequently confused with intentional acts in general, but as William James [1950] and Claparède [1951] have shown, will is useless when one already has a single, firm intention.

Will appears when there is a conflict of tendencies or tensions when, for example, one oscillates between a tempting pleasure and a duty. Then what does will consist of? In such a conflict, there is always an inferior tendency that, in and of itself, is stronger (the desire for pleasure, in this example) and a superior tendency that is momentarily weaker (the duty). The act of will does not consist of following the inferior and stronger tendency; on the contrary, one would then speak of a failure of will or "lack of will power." Will power involves reinforcing the superior but weaker tendency so as to make it triumph.

This problem is of great interest to the psychology of mental development as well, having an obvious bearing on what is called "the education of the will" [Payot, 1909]. The problem is to understand how the tendency that is weaker to start with (i.e., the superior tendency that risks being defeated by the inferior desire) becomes the stronger tendency because of an act of will. This, as William James (1950) has said, is an inexplicable "fiat." In reality, all the fundamental emotions linked to the activity of the individual betray regulations of energy. Interest, for example, which we mentioned in the discussion of early childhood (II C), is an astonishing regulator. It suffices to be interested in work in order to find the necessary strength to pursue it, whereas disinterest curtails the expenditure of energy. The system of interests or values, which changes at every moment depending on the activity in progress, thus incessantly commands the system of internal energies by means of a quasi-automatic and continuous regulating process. However, it is only what might be called an intuitive regulator, since it is partly irreversible and subject to frequent displacements of equilibrium. Will, on the other hand, is a regulation that has become reversible, and in this sense it is comparable to an operation. When a duty is momentarily weaker than a specific desire, will re-establishes values according to their pre-established hierarchy and ensures their subsequent conservation. Will gives primacy to the tendency of lesser strength by reinforcing it. Thus it acts exactly like the logical operation when the deduction (equivalent to the superior but weaker tendency) is at odds with a perceptual appearance (equivalent to the inferior but stronger tendency) and operational reasoning corrects actual [but misleading] appearances by referring to previous states. It is natural, therefore, that will should develop during the same period as the intellectual operations, while moral values become organized into autonomous systems comparable to logical groupings.

4. ADOLESCENCE

The preceding reflections might lead one to think that mental development is completed at eleven to twelve years of age and that adolescence is simply a temporary crisis, resulting from puberty, that separates the child from the adult. It is true that the maturation of the sexual instinct is marked by a momentary disequilibrium that lends a characteristic affective coloration to this last period of psychological evolution. But these well-known facts, made banal by certain psychological writings,[27] far from exhaust the analysis of adolescence. Indeed, pubertal changes would play only a very secondary role if the thinking and emotions characteristic of adolescents were accorded their true significance. We shall describe the structures of these final forms of thought and of the affective life, rather than the problems of adolescence. In addition, while there is provisional disequilibrium, one must not forget that every transition from one stage to another is likely to provoke temporary oscillations. In reality, appearance notwithstanding, adolescence assures thought and affectivity of an equilibrium superior to that which existed during middle and late childhood. Abilities multiply, and at first these additional capacities are troubling to both thought and affectivity, but subsequently they strengthen them.

For brevity's sake, we shall subsume the period of adolescence under two rubrics: thought, with its new operations; and affectivity, including social behavior.

A. Thought and Its Operations

By comparison with a child, an adolescent is an individual who constructs systems and "theories." The child does not build systems. Those which he possesses are unconscious or preconscious in the sense that they are unformulable or unformulated so that only an external observer can understand them, while he himself never "reflects" on them. In other words, he thinks concretely, he deals with each problem in isolation and does not integrate his solutions by means of any general theories from which he could abstract a common principle. By contrast, what is striking in the adolescent is his interest in theoretical problems not related to everyday realities. He is frequently occupied with disarmingly naïve and chimeric ideas concerning the future of the world. What is particularly surprising is his facility for elaborating abstract theories. Some write; they may create a philosophy, a political tract, a theory of aesthetics, or whatever. Others do not write; they talk. The majority talk only about a small part of their personal creations and confine themselves to ruminating about them intimately and in secret. But all of them have systems and theories that transform the world in one way or another.

The eruption of this new kind of thinking, in the form of general ideas and abstract constructions, is actually much less sudden than it would seem. It develops in relatively continuous fashion from the concrete thinking of middle childhood. The turning point occurs at about the age of twelve, after which there is rapid progress in the direction of free reflection no longer directly attached to external reality. At eleven or twelve years of age there is a fundamental transformation in the child's thinking which marks the completion of the operations constructed during middle childhood. This is the transition from concrete to "formal" thinking, or, in a barbarous but clear term, "hypothetico-deductive" thinking.

Up to this age (eleven–twelve), the operations of intelligence are solely "concrete," i.e., they are concerned only with reality itself and, in particular, with tangible objects that can be manipulated and subjected to real action. When at the concrete level, thinking moves away from tangible reality, absent objects are replaced by more or less vivid representations, which are tantamount to reality. If a child at this level is asked to reason about simple hypotheses, presented verbally, he immediately loses ground and falls back on the prelogical intuition of the preschool child. For example, all children of nine or ten can arrange colors into series even better than they can arrange sizes, yet they are completely unable to answer the following question, even when it is put in writing: "Edith has darker hair than Lily. Edith's hair is lighter than Susan's. Which of the three has the darkest hair?" [28] In general, they reply that since Edith and Lily are dark-haired and Edith and Susan are light-haired, Lily is the darkest, Susan the lightest, and Edith in between [Piaget, 1951(a)]. On the verbal plane, they succeed in producing only a series of uncoordinated pairs, as children of five or six do when they attempt to seriate a set of size-graded objects. That is why in school they have such difficulty in resolving arithmetic problems, even though such problems involve operations well known to them. If the children were able to manipulate objects, they would be able to reason without difficulty, whereas apparently the same reasoning on the plane of language and verbal statements actually constitutes other reasoning that is much more difficult because it is linked to pure hypotheses without effective reality.

As of eleven to twelve years, formal thinking becomes possible, i.e., the logical operations begin to be transposed from the plane of concrete manipulation to the ideational plane, where they are expressed in some kind of language (words, mathematical symbols, etc.), without the support of perception, experience, or even faith. In the previous example—"Edith has darker hair than Lily, etc."—three fictive personages are presented in the abstract as pure hypotheses, and thinking involves reasoning about these hypotheses. Formal thought is "hypothetico-deductive," in the sense that it permits one to draw conclusions from pure hypotheses and not merely from actual observations. These conclusions even have a validity independent of their factual truth. This explains why formal thinking represents so much more difficulty and so much more mental work than concrete thought.

What, in effect, are the conditions for the construction of formal thought? The child must not only apply operations to objects—in other words, mentally execute possible actions on them—he must also "reflect" these operations in the absence of the objects which are replaced by pure propositions. This "reflection" is thought raised to the second power. Concrete thinking is the representation of a possible action, and formal thinking is the representation of a representation of possible action. It is not surprising, therefore, that the system of concrete operations must be completed during the last years of childhood before it can be "reflected" by formal operations. In terms of their function, formal operations do not differ from concrete operations except that they are applied to hypotheses or propositions. Formal operations engender a "logic of propositions" in contrast to the logic of relations, classes, and numbers engendered by concrete operations. The system of "implications" that governs these propositions is merely an abstract translation of the system of "inference" that governs concrete operations.

Only after the inception of formal thought, at around the age of eleven or twelve, can the mental systems that characterize adolescence be constructed. Formal operations provide thinking with an entirely new ability that detaches and liberates thinking from concrete reality and permits it to build its own reflections and theories. With the advent of formal intelligence, thinking takes wings, and it is not surprising that at first this unexpected power is both used and abused. The free activity of spontaneous reflection is one of the two essential innovations that distinguish adolescence from childhood.

In accordance with a law we have already seen manifested in the infant and the young child, each new mental ability starts off by incorporating the world in a process of egocentric assimilation. Only later does it attain equilibrium through a compensating accommodation to reality. The intellectual egocentricity of adolescence is comparable to the egocentricity of the infant who assimilates the universe into his own corporal activity and to that of the young child who assimilates things into his own nascent thought (symbolic play, etc.). Adolescent egocentricity is manifested by belief in the omnipotence of reflection, as though the world should submit itself to idealistic schemes rather than to systems of reality. It is the metaphysical age *par excellence*; the self is strong enough to reconstruct the universe and big enough to incorporate it.

Then, just as the sensorimotor egocentricity of early childhood is progressively reduced by the organization of schemata of action and as the young child's egocentric thinking is replaced with the equilibrium of concrete operations, so the metaphysical egocentricity of the adolescent is gradually lessened as a reconciliation between formal thought and reality is effected. Equilibrium is attained when the adolescent understands that the proper function of reflection is not to contradict but to predict and interpret experience. This formal equilibrium surpasses by far the equilibrium of concrete thought because it not only encompasses the real world but also the undefined constructions of rational deduction and inner life.

B. The Affectivity of the Personality in the Social World of Adults

Exactly parallel to the elaboration of the formal operations and the completion of the constructions of thought, adolescent affectivity asserts itself through the development of the personality and its injection into adult society.

What is personality and why does it achieve its final form in adolescence? Psychologists are accustomed to making a distinction between the self and the personality and even to contrast them. The self, while it may not appear immediately, is at any rate relatively primitive. It is like the center of one's own activity and is characterized by its conscious or unconscious egocentricity. Personality, on the other hand, results from the submission, or rather the autosubmission, of the self to some kind of discipline. For example, a man is not said to have a strong personality when everything is egotistically determined and he remains incapable of dominating the self. He is said to have a strong personality when he incarnates an ideal or defends a cause with all his activity and will. It has even been said that personality is a social product linked to the role it plays in society (persona = theater mask). Personality implies cooperation and personal autonomy. It is opposed both to *anomie*, the complete absence of rules, and to complete heteronomy, abject submission to the constraints imposed from without.[29] In this sense, the person and the social relationships he engenders and maintains are interdependent.

Personality formation begins in middle to late childhood (eight to twelve years) with the autonomous organization of rules and values, and the affirmation of will with respect to the regulation and hierarchical organization of moral tendencies. But there is more to the person than these factors alone. These factors are integrated with the self into a unique system to which all the separate parts are subordinated. There is then a "personal" system in the dual sense that it is peculiar to a given individual and implies autonomous coordination. Now this personal system cannot be constructed prior to adolescence, because it presupposes the formal thought and reflexive constructions we have just discussed (see A). One might say that personality exists as soon as a "life plan" (*Lebensplan*),[30] which is both a source of discipline for the will and an instrument of cooperation, is formed. But this life plan presupposes the intervention of thought and free reflection, which is why it is not elaborated until certain intellectual conditions, such as the attainment of formal or hypothetico-deductive thought, are fulfilled.

Now personality implies a kind of decentering of the self which becomes part of a cooperative plan which subordinates itself to autonomous and freely constructed discipline. It follows that disequilibrium will recenter the self on itself, so that oscillations between the personality and the self are possible at all levels. Hence, in particular, the egocentricity of adolescence. We have already discussed the intellectual egocentricity of adolescence, and its affective aspects are well known. The young child unwittingly models the world in his own image but nonetheless feels inferior to adults and the older children whom he imitates. He thus fashions a kind of separate world at a level below the world of his elders. The adolescent, on the other hand, thanks to his budding personality, sees himself as equal to his elders, yet different from them, different because of the new life stirring within him. He wants to surpass and astound them by transforming the world. That is why the adolescent's systems or life plans are at the same time filled with generous sentiments and altruistic or mystically fervent projects and with disquieting megalomania and conscious egocentricity. In a discreet and anonymous inquiry into the daydreams of a class of fifteen-year-olds, a French teacher found future marshals of France or presidents of the Republic, great men of all kinds, among the most timid and serious boys, some of whom already saw their statues in the squares of Paris. In short, these were individuals, who, had they been thinking out loud, would have been suspected of paranoia. The diaries of adolescents also reveal the same constant mixture of devotion to humanity and acute egocentricity. The phenomenon is the same whether it has to do with the misunderstood and anxious youngster convinced of failure who questions the value of life itself or with the active youngster convinced of his own genius.

The synthesis of these projects of social cooperation and self-valuation signals the disequilibrium of the nascent personality and often appears as a form of Messianism. The adolescent in all modesty attributes to himself an essential role in the salvation of humanity and organizes his life plan accordingly. In this regard, it is interesting to note the transformations of religious feelings during the course of adolescence. As Bovet [1928] has demonstrated, religious feelings in early childhood start by being confused with filial feelings. The young child spontaneously attributes to his parents the diverse perfections of divinity, such as omnipotence, omniscience, and moral perfection. It is only when the child discovers the adult's imperfections that he sublimates his filial feelings by transferring them to the supernatural beings presented to him through religious education. But while an active mystical life is occasionally encountered toward the end of childhood, it is in general not until adolescence that real value is placed on integrating religion with the life systems whose beginnings we have already considered. The adolescent's religious feelings, however intense they may be (negative as well as positive), are frequently colored to a greater or lesser extent by messianic preoccupations. The adolescent makes a pact with his God, promising to serve him without return, but, by the same token, he counts on playing a decisive role in the cause he has undertaken to defend.

We see, then, how the adolescent goes about injecting himself into adult society. He does so by means of projects, life plans, theoretical systems, and ideas of political or social reform. In short, he does so by means of thinking and almost, one might say, by imagination—so far does this hypothetico-deductive thinking sometimes depart from reality. When adolescence is reduced to puberty, as though the rapid progress of the sexual instinct were the characteristic trait of this last stage of mental development, one sees only one aspect of the total change that characterizes this period. Certainly the adolescent does in a sense discover love. But is it not striking how often, even in cases where love finds a living object, love is simply the projection of an ideal onto a real being? Hence the disappointments that are as sudden and as symptomatic as falling in love. The adolescent loves in a void or practically so, as though he were in a novel, and the construction of this novel is perhaps more interesting than its instinctual content. Undoubtedly, the life plan of young girls is more closely linked to personal relationships, and their hypothetico-deductive systems take on the form more of a hierarchy of affective values than of a theoretical system. Nevertheless, they are also concerned with a life plan that goes far beyond reality. If their life plan is more concerned with people, this is because the life for which they are preparing is more concerned with specific interpersonal feelings than with general emotions.

In the adolescent's social life, as in other areas, there is an initial phase of "holding back" (Charlotte Bühler's [1931] negative phase) and a positive phase. During the first phase, the adolescent frequently appears asocial and practically asociable. Nothing, however, could be less true, since he is constantly meditating about society. The society that interests him is the society he wants to reform; he has nothing but disdain or disinterest for the real society he condemns. Furthermore, adolescent sociability develops through the young person's interactions with other adolescents. It is highly instructive to compare the social interaction of adolescents with that of children. The latter association has as its essential goal the collective game or, perhaps less frequently (because school organization does not take proper advantage of the situation), concrete common work. Adolescent social interaction, on the other hand, is aimed primarily at discussion. Whether in twosomes or in small coteries, the world is reconstructed in common, and the adolescent loses himself in endless discussion as a means of combating the real world. Sometimes there is mutual criticism of respective solutions, but there is general agreement as to the absolute necessity for reform. Then come broader interactions and young people's movements, where attempts at positive reorganization are made and great collective enthusiasms are exhibited.

True adaptation to society comes automatically when the adolescent reformer attempts to put his ideas to work. Just as experience reconciles formal thought with the reality of things, so does effective and enduring work, undertaken in concrete and well-defined situations, cure all dreams. One should not be disquieted by the extravagance and disequilibrium of the better part of adolescence. If specialized studies are not enough, once the last crises of adaptation have been surmounted, professional work definitely restores equilibrium and thus definitively marks the advent of adulthood. In general, individuals who, between the ages of fifteen and seventeen, never constructed systems in which their life plans formed part of a vast dream of reform or who, at first contact with the material world, sacrificed their chimeric ideals to new adult interests, are not the most productive. The metaphysics peculiar to the adolescent, as well as his passions and his megalomania, are thus real preparations for personal creativity, and examples of genius show that there is always continuity between the formation of personality, as of eleven to twelve years, and the subsequent work of the man.

This then is mental development. In conclusion, let us point out the basic unity of the processes which, from the construction of the practical universe by infantile sensorimotor intelligence, lead to the reconstruction of the world by the hypothetico-deductive thinking of the adolescent, via the knowledge of the concrete world derived from the system of operations of middle childhood. We have seen how these successive constructions always involve a decentering of the initial egocentric point of view in order to place it in an ever-broader coordination of relations and concepts, so that each new terminal grouping further integrates the subject's activity by adapting it to an ever-widening reality. Parallel to this intellectual elaboration, we have seen affectivity gradually disengaging itself from the self in order to submit, thanks to the reciprocity and coordination of values, to the laws of cooperation. Of course, affectivity is always the incentive for the actions that ensue at each new stage of this progressive ascent, since affectivity assigns value to activities and distributes energy to them. But affectivity is nothing without intelligence. Intelligence furnishes affectivity with its means and clarifies its ends. It is erroneous and mythical to attribute the causes of development to great ancestral tendencies as though activities and biological growth were by nature foreign to reason. In reality, the most profound tendency of all human activity is progression toward equilibrium. Reason, which expresses the highest forms of equilibrium, reunites intelligence and affectivity.

NOTES

[1] Originally published in *Juventus Helvetica*, 1940.

[2] The reference here is probably to Baldwin (1906), who defined the circular reaction as one "which is at once a new accommodation to any sort of stimulation and the beginning of a habit or tendency to get that sort of stimulation again." (*Op. cit.*, p. 264.) Ed.

[3] The research reported below (pp. 113–15) is from Piaget, 1954. Ed.

[4] Piaget may refer here, at least in part, to the work of Watson and Morgan (1917), who argued that love, rage, and fear were unlearned reactions. According to these writers, love was provoked in response to stroking, rage in response to physical restraint, and fear in response to loud noises and loss of support. Ed.

[5] The research which follows (pp. 19–21) is drawn from Piaget, 1952(b). Ed.

[6] The research which follows (pp. 24–25) is drawn mainly from Piaget, 1952(g). Ed.

[7] As becomes more evident later, Piaget seems here to be distinguishing between physical causality (mechanism) involving general laws, and psychological causality (teleology) involving intention and purpose. Ed.

[8] Two small mountains shaped like crocodiles that dominate the city of Geneva. Ed.

[9] The studies which follow (pp. 26–28) are largely from Piaget, 1951(b), 1951(c). Ed.

[10] Probably the deaf mute D'Estrella described by James (1892) in an early article. Ed.

[11] Piaget's choice of the phrase "prelogical" was unfortunate. Although Piaget meant only that the child before about the age of seven did not manifest a *complete* logical system, others took this phrase to mean that the young child was nonlogical or alogical. As the later essays show, Piaget has corrected this misunderstanding by referring to the young child as preoperational. The *pre*, however, must be taken literally to mean a stage prior to operations and preparatory to them and not as a stage entirely lacking in all evidences of logic. Ed.

[12] The study which follows (pp. 30–31) is reported more fully in Piaget, 1952(a).

[13] The studies below (pp. 31–32) are from Piaget, 1946(b). Ed.

[14] In French, as in English, the term "interest" has a twofold significance, depending upon whether it is used in the singular or the plural. In the singular it refers to a motivation or a striving on the part of the subject (interest) and in the plural to the objects of that striving (interests). Ed.

[15] The parallel between this conception and that of "level of aspiration" may not be accidental. Studies on level of aspiration were first introduced

by Hoppe (1930) and were in vogue in the late thirties and early forties when this article was written. For a summary of this research, cf. Lewin, 1954. Ed.

[16] This is true even when the child does not in fact obey, as is the case during that period of resistance which one often sees at three to four years of age and which German authors have called the "Trotzalter" (age of pride or spirit).

[17] The material on children's lies referred to on pages 37-38 is based on research reported in Piaget, 1948. Ed.

[18] The opinions expressed here parallel closely those of George Herbert Mead (1956), who contended that "thought . . . is only the importation of outer conversation, conversation with gestures, within the self in which the individual takes the role of others as well as his own role." (*Op. cit.*, p. 42.) Ed.

[19] Piaget probably refers here to the Milesian school of philosophy. Miletus was a commercial city of Iona (destroyed in 494 B.C. by the Persians) whose triad of philosophers was Thales, Anaximander, and Anaximenes. Thales held that everything could be reduced to water, whereas Anaximenes argued that the fundamental substance was air. Piaget deals with the parallels between the ideas of children and those of the pre-Socratics more fully in the article entitled "Children's Philosophies." (Piaget, 1931.) Ed.

[20] Piaget may well refer here to the Hegelian school of philosophy, in which all dichotomies, including that of cause and effect, could, by a higher-order synthesis, be subsumed under the principle of identity. Ed.

[21] The experiments which follow (pp. 43-46) were originally reported in Piaget and Inhelder, 1941. Ed.

[22] The reference for the study reported below (pp. 49-51) is Piaget, 1952(a). Ed.

[23] The reference for the following study (pp. 51-52) is Piaget and Inhelder, 1941. Ed.

[24] The reference for the study reported below (pp. 52) is Piaget, 1951(a). Ed.

[25] The experiment which follow, (pp. 52-53) are drawn from Piaget, 1952(a). Ed.

[26] Put differently, the argument is this. The concept of a unit is fundamental to a true or adult conception of number. The concept of a unit implies the union of the similarity and the difference relationships. A unit is like every other unit in the sense that it can be counted and different from every other in its order of enumeration. Only when the child can grasp that an element can at once be like and different from another can he arrive at a true unit, hence number, concept. Ed.

[27] Piaget may allude here, at least in part, to Hall's (1908) two-volume work on adolescence, in which the social difficulties encountered by young people were recounted in considerable detail. Ed.

[28] This test is taken from Burt (1913). It will be recalled that Piaget's interest in children as subjects was probably first stimulated in 1918 when, at the suggestion of Dr. Simon, he undertook to standardize the Burt tests on Parisian children. Ed.

[29] For a full development of a similar notion of relative autonomy, see Rapaport, 1951. Ed.

[30] Piaget himself constructed such a life plan as an adolescent and published it in the form of a novel. To a remarkable extent, Piaget has completed the program of work outlined in that early book, appropriately called *Recherches*. It should be noted, too, that the formal construction of such life plans is much more common in Europe than it is in America. Ed.

PART

Two

CHAPTER 2

The Thought of
the Young Child [1]

⟨⟩ MY FRIEND ELVIN,[2] whom I thank very much for the honor of inviting me to speak at your institute, has given me a very broad subject to discuss, no doubt in order to see how I would manage to dissect it. "The Thought of the Young Child" is an enormous subject, which I have studied for more than forty years without yet having covered it, and it may be approached from many points of view. I shall consider three of them:

1) Our studies show, first of all, in what respects the child differs from the adult, i.e., what the young child lacks in order to be able to reason like an average middle-class adult. It can be verified, for example, that certain logico-mathematical structures are not operative at all ages, hence are not innate.

2) Our studies show how cognitive structures are constructed. In this respect, child psychology may serve as an expository method for psychology in general, because to some extent the progressive formation of a structure furnishes its own explanation.

3) Our studies of the mode of construction of certain structures offers a response to certain questions posed by the philosophy of science. In this respect, child psychology can be extended into a "genetic epistemology."

1. THE CHILD AND THE ADULT

Let us start with the differences between the child and the adult. I maintained in my earlier books that the child began by being "prelogical," not in the sense of a fundamental heterogeneity between the child and the adult, but in the sense of the necessity for a progressive construction of the logical structures. This hypothesis has been widely criticized, especially in Great Britain, and above all because my arguments were drawn from verbal thought. For example, it has been pointed out by N. S. Isaacs [1930], among others (and in this respect with reason), that the child is more logical in action than in words. In general, I am little affected by critics, because they often do not understand an author's precise meaning when his contentions are far from accepted modes of thought,[2] but the service which critics render is to impel a more prudent and more thoroughgoing analysis of the data.

When I myself had children I was better able to understand the role of action in the development of intelligence. In particular, I learned that actions were the starting point for the future *operations* of intelligence. An operation is an internalized action which becomes reversible and is coordinated with other operations into an integrated operational grouping. However, since operations materialize only toward seven or eight years of age, there is a long "preoperational" period of development which corresponds to what I used to call the "prelogical" period. (Operations themselves are formed in two successive stages: the "concrete" stage between seven and eleven years of age, and the "formal" or propositional stage, which appears only at age eleven to twelve years.)

Returning to the observations of my own children, I subjected the observation of infantile behavior to the same analysis which I first employed with respect to verbal behavior. I obtained—in a much more primitive and essential form—some of the same results I had previously obtained through language alone. For example, I had maintained that the thought of the young child was egocentric, not in the sense of a hypertrophy of the self, but in the sense of centration on his own point of view. There seemed to be an initial lack of differentiation among points of view, which necessitated a differentiation by means of *decentration* in order to arrive at objectivity. The study of the sensorimotor development of space at levels prior to the acquisition of language led to exactly the same conclusions. Development begins by the construction of a multiplicity of heterogeneous spaces (oral, tactile, visual, etc.), each of which is centered on the child's own body or perspective. Then, after a kind of miniature Copernican revolution, space finally becomes a general place that contains all objects including the child's own body. It is in this way that space becomes decentered during infancy.

There is no basic difference between verbal logic and the logic inherent in the coordination of actions, but the logic of actions is more profound and more primitive. It develops more rapidly and surmounts the difficulties it encounters more quickly, but they are the same difficulties of decentration as those which will appear later in the field of language.

The most universal manner in which the initial logic of the child differs from our own (but with a lag between its manifestations in action and its manifestations in language) is undoubtedly its *irreversibility* due to the initial absence of decentration, hence its lack of *conservations*. In effect, the logicomathematical operations are, as we have seen, internalized, reversible actions (in the sense that each operation has an inverse, such as subtraction with respect to addition) coordinated into integrated groupings. The child first perceives by means of simple, one-way actions with centration on the *states* (and, above all, on the *final* states) without the decentration which alone permits the conceptualization of "transformations" as such. The basic consequence is that the conservation of objects, sets, quantities, etc., is not immediate before operational decentration is achieved. For example, a single object which leaves the perceptual field (hidden beneath a screen) only gradually acquires permanence at the sensorimotor level (eight to twelve months), and the number of objects in a collection whose form is modified is conserved, on the average, only toward seven or eight years.

The study of various forms of nonconservation, which we are still undertaking, shows that they do not result from a spontaneous tendency toward change (because the child is, on the contrary, above all a conservationist), but from an initial lack of reversible operations. For example, we [Piaget and Inhelder, 1963] have recently repeated and modified our early experiments on the nonconservation of liquid quantities (as this nonconservation is observed in the transfer of a liquid from receptacle A to a narrower and higher receptacle B). Before the transfer of liquids from one container A to another B, we first asked the subjects to anticipate (a) whether or not there would be conservation of the liquid and (b) how high the water would rise in receptacle B. Subjects from four to six years generally anticipated (a) that the quantity would remain the same, i.e., would be conserved, and (b) that the level itself was conserved. When the liquid was actually transferred, they were surprised to see that the level in receptacle B was higher than it was in A and, as a result, they concluded that there was nonconservation of the liquid quantity. It is true that certain children (very few) correctly predict the raised level in B (no doubt as a result of prior spontaneous experimentation) and then predict nonconservation. The following experiment clarifies these reactions. A child is given an empty glass A and a narrower empty glass B and is asked to pour liquid into A and into B so that there will be "the same amount to drink in each glass." The child will put exactly the same level of water into A and into B without bothering about the size of the glass. By contrast, after the age of six and a half to seven, the majority of children believe in the conservation of the liquid and can predict the difference in levels.

This repetition of early experiments shows that the basic

reason for nonconservation has to do with the fact that the young child reasons only about *states* or static configurations and neglects *transformations* as such. In order to conceptualize these transformations, one must reason by means of reversible "operations" and these are built up only little by little by means of a progressive regulation of the compensations involved.

2. THE COGNITIVE STRUCTURES

This leads us to the second part of our study. How do the logico-mathematical, operational structures become constructed? It seems to me that the study of this construction gives child psychology an explanatory value which is of interest to psychology as a whole, in the sense that the genesis (or successive development, since they do not have absolute beginnings) of these structures is linked to the causality of the formative mechanisms. It is regrettable that in certain circles child psychologists have no contact with experimentalists and experimental psychologists ignore the child; the genetic dimension is necessary to explication in general.

The logico-mathematical operations derive from actions themselves, because they are the product of an abstraction which proceeds from the coordination of actions and not from the objects themselves. For example, the operations of "order" derive from the coordination of actions. To discern a certain order in a series of objects or events one must be capable of registering this order through actions (from ocular movements to manual reconstitution) which must themselves be ordered. Objective order is learned only through an order inherent in the actions themselves. A learning theorist, D. Berlyne, who worked with us for a year on experiments dealing with, among other things, the learning of order, found that to "learn" order, one must have a "counter" at one's disposition, which is equivalent to what I call an ordinated activity. [Cf. Berlyne and Piaget, 1960.]

These operations are not, however, merely internalized ac-

tions. For operations to exist, these actions must become reversible and capable of being coordinated into integrated structures
which can be expressed in such general algebraic terms as:
"groupings," "groups," "lattices," etc.

The construction of structures is often effected in a complex
and unexpected manner, as is demonstrable, for example, in the
conceptualization of whole numbers. We studied this problem
some time ago and have recently reverted to it.

We know that mathematicians hold two major types of
hypotheses with respect to the construction of the whole numbers. On the one hand, according to the "intuitionists" (Poincaré [1908], Brouwer [1949], etc.), number is constructed independently of logical structures and results from operational
"intuitions" which are relatively primitive, such as the intuition
of "n + 1." On the other hand, there are those who hypothesize
that numerical structures are derived from logical structures.
For example, in *Principia Mathematica*, Whitehead and Russell [1910; 1912; 1913] seek to reduce the cardinal number to
the concept of class and the ordinal number to that of a
transitive asymmetric relationship.

The psychological facts, however, do not accord with either
of these hypotheses. In the first place, they show that all the
elements of the number are logical in nature. There is no
intuition of "n + 1" before a conservation of sets, based on
operational inclusions (classifications) or seriations, is constructed. In the second place, these logical constituents give rise
to a new synthesis in the case of the whole number, a synthesis
which does not correspond to a simple composition of classes or
to a simple serial composition but to both together. We are not
dealing with a simple composition of classes, because if the
qualities are abstracted (which is necessary in order to obtain a
number) a factor of order (seriation) must be employed so that
the units, which are now identical, can be distinguished. In
addition, if the qualities are abstracted, the one-by-one correspondence which Russell employs for constructing class-by-class
equivalencies, is no longer a qualified correspondence (a

qualified element corresponding to another element of the same quality) but a unit correspondence which is already numerical, hence is begging the question. In short, the whole number is neither a simple system of class inclusions, nor a simple seriation, but an indissociable synthesis of inclusion and seriation. The synthesis derives from the abstraction of qualities and from the fact that these two systems (classification and seriation), which are distinct when their qualities are conserved, become fused as soon as their qualities are abstracted.

This construction of number seems somewhat heterodox from the point of view of logic, and the mathematician who did the English translation of my book, *The Child's Conception of Number* [1952(a)] asked me to delete from the English edition the formulas I had given at the end of the French edition because they seemed shocking to him and to English logicians. However, recently, an excellent logician, J. B. Grize [1961] provided a formalization of this psychological construction of the number which I had formulated through simple observation of the child. He presented it to our Symposia of The Center for the Study of Genetic Epistemology and logicians such as E. W. Beth and W. V. O. Quine, who were present at the Symposia, saw no problems in it except with respect to some possible ameliorations of detail. Thus a new explanation of the elaboration of number has been furnished by child psychology. Genetic psychology is therefore instructive not only with regard to the ways in which the child differs from the adult but also with regard to the construction of certain logico-mathematical structures which finally form a part of all the evolved forms of adult thought.

3. PSYCHOLOGY AND GENETIC EPISTEMOLOGY

A few final remarks remain to be made. In certain instances, the genetic study of the construction of concepts and operations provides a response to questions posed by the sciences with respect to their methods of knowledge. When this is the case, child psychology becomes extended into a "genetic episte-mology."

I shall give one example, that of time and speed. At a philosophy of science meeting in 1928, Einstein asked me if, from a psychological point of view, the concept of speed developed as a function of time or whether it was built up independently of all duration or was even more primitive than the concept of duration. We know that in classical mechanics the concept of speed depends on' duration, whereas from the relativist point of view, duration, by contrast, depends on speed. We therefore went to work, and our findings with respect to the development of the concept of speed were used by two French relativists in a new formulation of the concepts of speed and time.

Let us start with the concept of time. Time is manifested in two ways: through the successive order of events and the duration or interval between ordered events. In the young child it is easy to see that the estimation of ordinal relations (succession or simultaneity) depends on speed [Piaget, 1946(a)]. For example, if two mannikins are set off at the same speed from the same line of departure on two parallel routes, the child will have no difficulty in recognizing that their respective departures and arrivals will be simultaneous. However, if one of the mannikins goes faster and thus arrives at a point farther away, the child will say that the departures are simultaneous but that the mannikins do not stop "at the same time." This is not a perceptual error, since the child recognizes that when one of the mannikins stops, the other does not continue.

Simultaneity does not make sense to the child in this instance, because he does not yet understand the "same time" concept for two movements of unequal speed. At around the age of six, on the average, the child will accept the simultaneity of arrival as well as departure, but from this he does not conclude that the durations of the trips were the same, since it seems to him that a longer route must require more time owing to his inability to coordinate simultaneity and temporal intervals. Analogous observations can be made with respect to psychological time (slow and fast work, etc.). Time appears to be a coordination of movements, inclusive of speeds ($t = d:s$), just as space is based on a coordination of displacements; i.e., movements independent of their speed.

As for the concept of speed, the classical formula $s = d:t$ makes sense if the duration t and the distance covered d correspond to simple intuitions which exist prior to the concept of speed. However, we have just seen that the estimation of duration t begins by depending on speed. Is there, then, an intuition of speed which is anterior to duration or at least independent of it? The intuition of speed is, in fact, found in the child in the form of an ordinal intuition based on overtaking. A moving object is judged to be more rapid than another when at a given moment the first object is behind and a moment or so later ahead of the other object. The intuition of overtaking is based on the temporal order (before and after) and on the spatial order (behind and in front), but it is not based on duration or on the distance traversed. Nevertheless, it furnishes an exact criterion of speed. At first, the child considers only the points of arrival, and thus for a long time he makes errors with respect to simple overtaking or partial overtaking. However, when he becomes adept at anticipating the course of perceived movements and of generalizing the concept of overtaking, he acquires an original ordinal concept of speed [Piaget, 1950]. It is also interesting to note that the perception of speed stems from the same ordinal relations and necessitates no reference to duration [Piaget, Feller, and McNear, 1959].

The results of this research, which was inspired by Einstein, were then utilized in the field of relativity. This occurred in the following manner. We know that in physics, even in relativistic physics, there is difficulty in defining duration and speed without running into a vicious circle. Speed is defined with reference to duration ($s = d:t$), and one can measure duration only by means of speed (astronomics, mechanics, etc.) Now two French physicists have tried to avoid this vicious circle in their reformulation of the theory of relativity by using our findings on the psychological formation of the concept of speed. Using our work on the genesis of this concept in the child, they developed the theory of ordinal speed or overtaking. With the help of a logarithmic law and an Abelian group, they constructed a theorem of addition of speeds, and from this they arrived at the Lorenz group and the initial principles of the theory of relativity [Abele and Malvaux, 1954].

The young child's thinking manifests considerable activity that is frequently original and unpredictable. It is remarkable not only by virtue of the way it differs from adult thinking but also by virtue of what it teaches us about the way in which rational structures are formed. Sometimes this may even lead to the clarification of certain obscure aspects of scientific thought.

NOTES

[1] Lecture given at the Institute of Education, University of London, 1963.

[2] Herbert Lionel Elvin, Director of the University of London Institute of Education. Ed.

[3] For example, in an interesting work which will appear soon in English and in French on causal thinking in the child, two Canadian psychologists, M. Laurendeau and A. Pinard, replicated experiments which I used to analyze childhood "precausality" [Piaget, 1951(b)]. In a statistically evaluated study of five hundred children from four to twelve years of age, they verified the essential parts of my results. In addition, they wrote a taut criticism of all previous work on the same subject, much of which was critical of my hypotheses. Laurendeau and Pinard established that the divergences among these writers were due to two essential factors. One was that certain authors adopted criteria very different from my own. (Deutsche [1937], for example, included in his "materialist," as opposed to precausal, explanations a number of important phenomenal explanations which I classed as precausal.) The other factor (and this is even more significant) is that the experimenters used two different methods of examination, one based on the diverse responses of the same child, the other based on diverse responses to objects (regardless of the consistency peculiar to each child). It thus goes without saying that the writers who adopted the second method were in disagreement with me, whereas those who adopted the first method of analysis (which I employed) obtained the same results! [The book to which Piaget refers has since appeared, cf. Laurendeau and Pinard, 1962. Ed.]

CHAPTER 3

Language and Thought from the Genetic Point of View [1]

𝄢 THE FOLLOWING PAGES contain some of my personal views concerning the role of language in the formation of intelligence generally and of logical operations in particular. My remarks concerning the relationship between language and thought will be grouped according to three age periods: (1) the age period during which language is first acquired; (2) the age period during which emerge concrete logical operations (certain operations common to the logic of classes and of relations and applied, from seven to eleven years of age, to manipulable things); (3) the period during which formal or interpropositional operations are acquired (propositional logic is achieved between the ages of twelve and fifteen).

1. THOUGHT AND THE SYMBOLIC FUNCTION

When a child of two to three years in possession of elementary verbal expressions is compared with a baby of eight to ten months whose intelligence is still sensorimotor in nature, i.e., whose intellectual instruments consist of only percepts and movements, it seems at first glance that language has profoundly changed this initial intelligence of action by adding thinking to it. Thanks to language, the child has become capable of evoking absent situations and of liberating himself from the frontiers of immediate space and time, i.e., from the limits of the perceptual field, whereas sensorimotor intelligence is almost entirely confined within these frontiers. Also, thanks to language, objects and events are no longer experienced only in their perceptual immediacy; they are experienced within a conceptual and rational framework which enriches the understanding of them. In short, if the child's behavior prior to language is compared with his behavior after the inception of language, it is tempting to conclude, with Watson [1919] and many others, that language is the source of thought.

A closer examination, however, of the changes which occur in intelligence when language is acquired shows that language alone is not responsible for these transformations. The two essential innovations which we have just mentioned can be considered as the beginning of representation and of representative schematization (concepts, etc.), by contrast with sensorimotor schematization, which is concerned with actions themselves or with perceptual forms. There are sources other than language capable of explaining certain representations and certain representative schematizations. Language is necessarily interpersonal and is composed of a system of *signs* ("arbitrary" or conventional signifiers). But besides language, the small child, who is less socialized than he is after the age of seven to eight years and much less so than the adult, needs another system of signifiers which are more individual and more "motivated." These are the *symbols* which are most commonly found in the symbolic or imaginative play of the young child. Symbolic play appears at about the same time as language but independently of it and is of considerable significance in the young child's thinking. It is a source of personal cognitive and affective representations and of equally personal representative schematizations. For example, the first symbolic play observed in one of my children consisted of his pretending to sleep. In order to go to sleep he always held a corner of his pillowcase in his hand and put the thumb of the same hand into his mouth. One morning, sitting wide awake on his mother's bed, Laurent noticed a corner of the sheet and it reminded him of the corner of his pillowcase. He grabbed the corner of the sheet firmly in his hand, put his thumb in his mouth, closed his eyes, and while still sitting, smiled broadly. Here we have an example of a representation independent of language but attached to a ludic[2] symbol, which consists of appropriate gestures imitating those which ordinarily accompany a predetermined action. Action thus represented is not related to the present or the actual; it refers to an evoked context or situation, which is the hallmark of "representation."

Symbolic play is not the only form of personal symbolism. Another form emerges during the same period and also plays an important role in the genesis of representation. This is "deferred imitation" or imitation that occurs for the first time in the absence of the model to which it corresponds. For example, one of my daughters, while entertaining a small friend, was surprised to see him become angry, then cry and bang his feet. She did not react in his presence, but after his departure she imitated the scene without any sign of anger on her part.

Thirdly, all mental imagery can be classed among personal symbols. We know now that the image is neither an element of thought itself nor a direct continuation of perception. It is a symbol of the object which is not yet manifested at the level of sensorimotor intelligence (otherwise the solution of many practical problems would be much easier). The image can be conceived as an internalized imitation. The sonorous image is merely the internal imitation of its correspondent and the visual image is the product of an imitation of an object or of a person, either by the whole body or by ocular movements in the case of a small figure.

The three types of personal symbols we have cited (we might add dream symbols, but this would involve too long a discussion) are derived from [motor] imitation. This then is one of the possible links between sensorimotor behavior and representative behavior. It is independent of language, even though it aids in the acquisition of language.

We can say, therefore, that a symbolic function exists which is broader than language and encompasses both the system of verbal signs and that of symbols in the strict sense. It can thus be argued that the source of thought is to be sought in the symbolic function. But it can just as legitimately be maintained that the symbolic function itself is explained by the formation of representations. In fact, the essence of the symbolic function lies in the differentiation of the signifiers (signs and symbols) from the signified (objects or events that are schematic or conceptualized). In the sensorimotor realm, systems of signification already exist, since all perception and all cognitive adaptation consist of conferring significations (forms, ends and means, etc.). But the only signifier known to sensorimotor behavior is the *index* (as opposed to signs and symbols) or the *signal* (conditioned behavior).[3] Now the index and the signal are signifiers that are relatively undifferentiated from what they signify. They are actually merely parts or aspects of what is signified and not representations permitting their evocation. They lead to what is signified in the way that a part leads to the whole or the means to the ends and not as a sign or a symbol which permits the evocation (through thought) of an absent object or event. The symbolic function, on the other hand, consists of differentiating the signifiers from what is signified so that the former can permit the evocation of the representation of the latter. To ask whether the symbolic function engenders thought or thought permits the formation of symbolic function is as vain as to try to determine whether the river orients its banks or the banks orient the river.

As language is only a particular form of the symbolic function and as the individual symbol is certainly simpler than the collective sign, it is permissible to conclude that thought precedes language and that language confines itself to profoundly transforming thought by helping it to attain its forms of equilibrium by means of a more advanced schematization and a more mobile abstraction.

2. LANGUAGE AND THE "CONCRETE" LOGICAL OPERATIONS

But is language the only source of certain particular forms of thought, such as logical thought? The thesis of numerous logicians (the Vienna circle, Anglo-Saxon logical empiricists, etc.) is well known concerning the linguistic nature of logic conceived as a syntax and general semantics. But here again genetic psychology allows us to place in proper perspective certain theses which are exclusively derived from the examination of adult thought.

The first lesson to be learned from the study of the formation of logical operations in the child is that they are not constructed all at once but rather are elaborated in two successive stages. The propositional operations (propositional logic) with their particular groupings, such as those of the lattice and the group of four transformations (identity, inversion, reciprocity, and correlativity), do not appear until around eleven to twelve years of age and do not become systematically organized until between twelve and fifteen. By contrast, as of age seven or eight, systems of logical operations do not yet bear on propositions as such but on the classes and relations of objects themselves; and they are organized apropos of the real or imagined manipulation of these objects. This first set of operations, which we shall call "concrete operations," involves only the additive and multiplicative operations upon classes and relations which result in classifications, seriations, correspondences, etc. These operations do not cover the logic of classes and relations in its entirety but only the elementary "groupings," such as the semilattices and imperfect logical groups.

The problem of the relationship between language and thought can thus be posed in terms of these concrete opera-

tions. Is language the only source of the classifications, seriations, etc., which characterize the form of thought linked to
these operations, or, on the contrary, are the latter relatively
independent of language? Here is a highly simplified example.
All birds (class A) are animals (class B), but all animals are
not birds, because there are nonbird animals (class A'). The
problem, then, is whether the operations $A + A' = B$ and
$A = B - A'$ derive from language alone, which allows for the
grouping of objects into classes, A, A', and B, or whether these
operations have roots that lie deeper than language. An analogous problem can be posed with respect to the seriation:
$A < B < C < \ldots$ etc.

Now the study of the development of operations in the child
permits one to make a highly instructive observation. This is
that the operations which make possible the combination or the
dissociation of classes or relations are actions prior to their
becoming operations of thought. Before he can combine or
dissociate relatively universal and abstract classes, such as the
classes of birds or of animals, the child can already classify
collections of objects in the same perceptual field; he can combine or dissociate them manually before he can do so linguisti-
cally. By the same token, before he can seriate objects evoked
by means of language alone (as, for example, in Burt's [1913]
test: "Edith is blonder than Susan and darker than Lily; who is
the darkest of the three?"), the child can construct a series if,
for example, he is given a set of rulers graduated as to length.
The operations $+$, $-$, etc., are thus coordinations among actions before they are transposed into verbal form, so that language cannot account for their formation. Language indefinitely
extends the power of these operations and confers on them a
mobility and a universality which they would not have otherwise, but it is by no means the source of such coordinations.

We are at present conducting research in collaboration with
Miss Inhelder and Miss Affolter in order to determine which of
the mechanisms proper to the concrete operations subsist in the
thinking of deaf-mutes. It appears that the fundamental opera-

tions inherent in classification and seriation are more widely represented here than is generally believed. No doubt it could be rejoined that the deaf-mute has a language of gestures and that the young child who constructs classifications and seriations in action has also acquired spoken language which can then be transformed into these manipulations.

It suffices, however, to look at the sensorimotor intelligence which exists prior to the acquisition of language in order to find in the infant's elementary practical coordinations the functional equivalents of the operations of combination and dissociation. If a twelve-to-twenty-four-month-old baby sees a watch placed under a blanket and then, when he looks for it, finds instead a beret or a hat (under which the watch has been hidden), he immediately lifts up the beret and expects to find the watch.⁴ Thus he understands, in action, a sort of transitivity of relations which might be explained verbally as follows: "The watch was under the hat; the hat was under the blanket; therefore the watch is under the blanket." Such transitivity of actions constitutes the functional equivalent of what, on the representational plane, will be the transitivity of serial relations or topological nestings and even the inclusions of classes. Language makes these structures more universal and mobile than the sensorimotor coordinations, but where do the constitutive operations of representational nestings derive from if their roots do not reach down to the sensorimotor coordinations themselves? A large number of comparable examples demonstrates that these coordinations comprise, in actions, combinations and dissociations functionally comparable to the future operations of thought.

3. LANGUAGE AND PROPOSITIONAL LOGIC

While it is comprehensible that the concrete operations of classes and relations stem from acts of combination and dissociation, it may be argued that the propositional operations (i.e., those which characterize propositional logic) are, by contrast, an authentic product of language itself. In effect, the implications, disjunctions, incompatibilities, etc., which characterize propositional logic only appear at about eleven to twelve years. At this level reasoning becomes hypothetico-deductive; it is liberated from its concrete attachments and comes to rest on the universal and abstract plane for which only verbal thought appears to furnish the necessary generative conditions.

We certainly do not deny the considerable role language plays in the formation of such operations. But the question is not simply whether language is a necessary condition for the formation of formal operations. To that proposition we naturally concede. The question is also whether language is sufficient in and of itself to give rise to these operations *ex nihilo* or whether, on the contrary, its role is limited to allowing the fulfillment of structuring which originates from the systems of concrete operations and, therefore, from the wellsprings of action itself.

In order to grasp the psychology of operations peculiar to propositional logic, one should not address himself to the logistic axiomatization of propositions or to a simple enumeration of their isolable operations. The fundamental psychological reality which characterizes such operations is the integrated grouping which unites them in the same system and defines their algebraic utilization (the "calculus" of propositions).

While the formal grouping is complex, it is nonetheless undissociably bound to the concrete operational structures found in middle childhood. This formal grouping consists, first of all, of a "lattice," in the algebraic sense of the term.

The psychological problem in the formation of propositional operations consists of determining how the subject passes from elementary concrete structures (classifications, seriations, double entry matrices, etc.) to the structure of the lattice. The answer to this question is simple. What distinguishes a lattice from a simple classification (such as zoological classifications, for example) is the intervention of combinatory operations. Thus the sixteen binary operations which can be constructed with two propositions p and q result from one combination. The four basic associations $(p \cdot q)$, $(p \cdot \bar{q})$, $(\bar{p} \cdot q)$, $(\bar{p} \cdot \bar{q})$ are isomorphic to what would be produced by a simple multiplication of classes $(P + \bar{P}) \times (Q + \bar{Q}) = PQ + P\bar{Q} + \bar{P}Q + \bar{P}\bar{Q}$, hence to an operation already accessible to subjects of seven to eight years. But the innovation peculiar to the propositional operations is that these four basic associations, which we shall call 1, 2, 3, and 4, give rise to sixteen combinations: 1, 2, 3, 4, 12, 13, 14, 23, 24, 34, 123, 124, 134, 234, 1234, and 0.

The question, then, is to ascertain whether language makes such combinatory operations possible or whether the operations evolve independently of language. Genetic facts leave no doubt as to the reply. Professor Inhelder's [Inhelder and Piaget, 1958] experiments on experimental reasoning and the induction of physical laws by adolescents, as well as the preceding research by Professor Inhelder and the writer [Piaget and Inhelder, 1951] on the development of combinatory operations show that these operations are constituted at about eleven to twelve years in all fields at once and not only on the verbal plane. For example, if subjects are asked to combine three or four different-colored discs according to all the combinations possible, up to eleven to twelve years the combinations remain incomplete and are constructed unsystematically, whereas from then on the subject manages to construct a complete and methodical system. It would be difficult to maintain that this system is a product of the evolution of language. On the contrary, the acquisition of combinatory operations permits the subject to complete his verbal classifications and to make these correspond to the abstract relationships inherent in the propositional operations.

Another aspect of the formal grouping of propositional operations is the "group" of the following four commutative transformations: for each propositional operation—e.g., the implication (p, q)— there is a corresponding inverse $N(p, \bar{q})$, a reciprocal $R(q, p)$ and a correlative $C(\bar{p}, q)$. Together with the identical transformation I, we have: $CN = R$; $CR = N$; $RN = C$; and $RNC = I$.

Of these four transformations the two principal ones are inversion or negation N and reciprocity R. The correlative C is none other than the reciprocal of the inverse (RN = C) or, which amounts to the same thing, the inverse of the reciprocal (NR = C). The question then is, once again, whether language brings about this coordination of transformations by inversion and by reciprocity or whether the transformations exist prior to their verbal expression and language is limited to facilitating their use and coordination.

Here, once again, the examination of genetic facts furnishes a reply which is oriented much more in the direction of an interaction between linguistic mechanisms and the subjacent operational mechanisms than in the direction of linguistic determinism.

Inversion and reciprocity are rooted in soil which antedates their symbolic function and which is, properly speaking, sensorimotor in nature. Inversion or negation is none other than an elaborated form of processes which are found at all levels of development. The baby already knows how to use an object as a means to attain a goal, as well as how to get rid of it as an obstacle in order to reach a new goal. The origins of this transformation by inversion or negation can be seen in the mechanisms of neural inhibition—for example, withdrawing the hand and arm after having stretched them out in a certain direction, etc. Reciprocity also extends to perceptual and motor symmetries, which are just as precocious as the preceding mechanisms.

While the parallel history of the diverse forms of inversion and reciprocity can be followed throughout the course of mental development, their coordination, i.e., their integration into a single system which implicates them both, is effected only at the level of propositional operations with the advent of the INRC "group" just described. It would be difficult to maintain that this coordination was due to language alone. This coordination is due to the construction of the grouping which participates both in the "lattice" and the "group" and engenders the propositional operations; it is not due to the verbal expression of these operations. In other words, this coordination is at the source of the operations and does not constitute their end product.

In the three domains we have just covered in broad outline, we have noted that language is not enough to explain thought, because the structures that characterize thought have their roots in action and in sensorimotor mechanisms that are deeper than linguistics. It is also evident that the more the structures of thought are refined, the more language is necessary for the achievement of this elaboration. Language is thus a necessary but not a sufficient condition for the construction of logical operations. It is necessary because without the system of symbolic expression which constitutes language the operations would remain at the stage of successive actions without ever being integrated into simultaneous systems or simultaneously encompassing a set of interdependent transformations. Without language the operations would remain personal and would consequently not be regulated by interpersonal exchange and cooperation. It is in this dual sense of symbolic condensation and social regulation that language is indispensable to the elaboration of thought. Thus language and thought are linked in a genetic circle where each necessarily leans on the other in interdependent formation and continuous reciprocal action. In the last analysis, both depend on intelligence itself, which antedates language and is independent of it.

NOTES

[1] Originally published in *Acta Psychologica*, 1959, XV, 51–62.

[2] This is not an entirely correct statement of Bertalanffy's position. What Bertalanffy (1952) seems to argue is that the second law of thermodynamics holds only for closed systems and that to account for open systems and "steady states" a new thermodynamics must be constructed. Ed.

[3] These studies have been summarized by Piaget in *Les Mécanismes perceptifs* (1961), Chapter 4. Ed.

[4] For this reason, if focusing upon one of the characteristics has a probability of $1/n$ and the other a probability of $1/m$, the probability of both together for a subject who assumes they are independent will be $1/nm < 1/n$ and $< 1/m$.

The Role of the Concept of Equilibrium in Psychological Explication[1]

PRACTICALLY ALL SCHOOLS of psychology have recourse to the concept of equilibrium and assign it a role in the explication of behavior. P. Janet [1929] invoked this concept in his theory of affective regulations, and Freud [1938] used it in similar fashion. Claparède [1951] considered need as the expression of disequilibrium and satisfaction as an index of re-equilibration. The succession of behavior appears to him like a succession of momentary disequilibriums and of re-establishments of equilibrium. Gestalt theory has extended this mode of interpretation to the cognitive structures (perception and intelligence) and K. Lewin [1935] has developed it in social psychology, notably through his use of topographical theory. Learning theory and conditioning naturally encounter the problem of equilibrium with respect to the stabilization of behavior. As for developmental theory in general, we ourselves have constantly had recourse to the concept of equilibrium in order to explain the genesis of operational structures and the transition from preoperational regulations to operations as such.

There are two major problems with respect to the concept of equilibrium: (1) what equilibrium explains and its role in psychological explication, and (2) how equilibrium itself is explained, i.e., what is the most adequate model to account for a process of equilibration?

We shall examine these two problems successively. In order to avoid all misunderstanding and at the risk of anticipating the second part of this essay, we shall immediately stipulate that we by no means conceive psychological equilibrium in the manner of a balance of forces in a state of rest but shall define it very broadly as the compensation resulting from the activities of the subject in response to external intrusion. It follows that equilibrium thus defined is compatible with the concept of an open system, and it would perhaps be better to speak—along with L. V. Bertalanffy [1960]—of a "stable state in an open system." But the term equilibrium nonetheless seems preferable in that it implies the idea of compensation. We must insist emphatically on the fact that external intrusion can be compensated only by activities. The maximum equilibrium will not involve a state of rest but rather a maximum of activity on the part of the subject, which will compensate both for the actual intrusion and for the virtual intrusion. The latter form of compensation is essential and must be underlined immediately, especially at the level of operational thought, where the subject attains equilibrium to the extent that he is capable of anticipating intrusion by representing it to himself through what we call "direct" operations and by compensating for it in advance by "inverse" operations.

What is important for psychological explication is not equilibrium as a state but, rather, the actual process of equilibration. Equilibrium is only a result, whereas the process as such has greater expository value.

In what follows we shall be concerned only with cognitive mechanisms and shall neglect affective factors (motivation), not as a matter of principle but in order to confine ourselves to what we have studied experimentally.

1. THE EXPLICATIVE ROLE OF THE CONCEPT OF EQUILIBRIUM

It should be noted first that equilibrium is not an extrinsic or added characteristic but rather an intrinsic and constitutive property of organic and mental life. A pebble may be in states of stable, unstable, or indifferent equilibrium with respect to its surroundings and this makes no difference to its nature. By contrast, an organism presents, with respect to its milieu, multiple forms of equilibrium, from postures to homeostasis. These forms are necessary to its life, hence are intrinsic characteristics; durable disequilibria constitute pathological organic or mental states.

The organism has special organs of equilibrium. The same is true of mental life, whose organs of equilibrium are special regulatory mechanisms. This is so at all levels of development, from the elementary regulations of motivation (needs and interests) up to will for affectivity and from perceptual and sensorimotor regulations up to operations for cognition. We shall see that the role of operations is to anticipate the intrusions which modify all of the representative systems and to compensate for them. This is accomplished by the complete reversibility which characterizes operational mechanisms, as opposed to the semireversibility of the regulational mechanisms of preoperational thought.

Consideration of the problems of equilibrium is, then, indispensable to biological and psychological explication. We shall not detail this necessity with respect to learning theories, since it is self-evident. It is self-evident because learning is characterized as a durable—and hence equilibrated—modification of behavior as a function of experience. Since it is not certain that the current learning theories are applicable to the acquisition of higher cognitive processes and since it is evident that learning constitutes only one aspect of development, we shall take development as our point of departure.

Unfortunately, the theory of development has been much less elaborated than that of learning because the former has collided with the fundamental difficulty of dissociating internal (maturational) factors from external (environmental) factors. This difficulty, however, is also instructive, as we shall see. The three classical factors in development are heredity, the physical environment, and the social environment. Behavior attributable entirely to maturation or entirely to environmental influences has never been observed. The same is true of biology. There is no genotype, even in a pure culture, which is not incarnated in various phenotypes (for the genotype is what is common to all the corresponding phenotypes and is not a reality to be placed on the same plane as the phenotypes). At the same time, there is no phenotype which is not related to a genotype or to a mixture of genotypes. If this fundamental interaction between internal and external factors is taken into account, all behavior is an *assimilation* of reality to prior schemata (schemata which, in varying degrees, are due to heredity) and all behavior is at the same time an *accommodation* of these schemata to the actual situation. The result is that developmental theory necessarily calls upon the concept of equilibrium, since all behavior tends toward assuring an equilibrium between internal and external factors or, speaking more generally, between assimilation and accommodation.

That is not all. Equilibrium should, in reality, be considered as a fourth factor along with the three preceding factors (maturation and the physical and social environment). It constitutes a fourth factor first of all because it is more general than the first three and also because it can be analyzed in a relatively autonomous manner. This autonomy does not signify that equilibration is independent of the other factors, since there is continuous interaction among them, but that it stems from particular modes of interpretation based on purely probabilistic considerations. For example, to the extent that the second principle of thermodynamics is applicable to vital phenomena (and Bertalanffy [1952] has shown that it does not contradict the concept of an open system or the growing differentiation of organic structures),[2] the growth of entropy can be considered neither as an innate mechanism nor as a physical or, above all, social acquisition. We have to do, instead, with a particular form of statistical or probabilistic causality, based on the interdependence of phenomena. No doubt, explications of this kind will be more arbitrary than those stemming from classic linear causality, but they will be independent of analysis according to the three other factors.

A serious objection nonetheless remains possible. In maintaining that development consists of a progressive equilibration, one is up against the dual difficulty that development appears like a succession of unstable states to the end of the genetic series and that even then the stable states remain exceptional. It could therefore be maintained that the equilibrium explication covers only an extremely limited area which reduces, in fact, to the logico-mathematical structures. The latter, once constructed, do in fact remain stable throughout life. For example, the succession of whole numbers, the logical structure of classes, of relations, and of propositions do not become modified even though they may become integrated into more complex structures. They draw their roots from mental life and reach fulfillment in social life; once elaborated, they constitute striking models of equilibrium both in social history and in individual development. It might thus be supposed that the concept of cognitive equilibrium is applicable only to particular instances, in contrast to the broad mass of intellectual processes in perpetual disequilibrium (since every problem, whether theoretical or practical, manifests the existence of a lacuna, i.e., of a disequilibrium).

This objection is valid only if the logico-mathematical operations are given a limited interpretation and considered as late developing and restricted in application. It is quite different if they are recognized as the final outcome of a general process of equilibration stemming from prelogical structures (sensorimotor, perceptual, and representative regulations of a preoperational level) but partially isomorphic to logic.

There are two possible psychological interpretations of the logico-mathematical structures. According to the first interpretation (which is empirically inspired), these structures derive from coordinations that appear after the event and that apply to independently discovered contents. From this point of view, a set of understandings resulting from perception, etc., acquired without the aid of logic, would first be elaborated. Only then would the logico-mathematical coordinations of these preliminary contents take place. According to the second interpretation (which is rationally or dialectically inspired), it would be impossible to discover any content without a structuring involving at least a partial isomorphism with logic. In this case the logico-mathematical structures, as well as their prelogical and premathematical forerunners, would be the instruments for acquiring understanding and not merely after-the-fact coordinations.

We can see the consequences of these two kinds of interpretation with respect to the problem of equilibrium. According to the first interpretation, logical structures are late-developing coordinations, different in origin from the formative processes of understanding that explain their own equilibrium. In this case, the concept of equilibrium would be subordinated to that of the coordinating structure and would lose its explanatory value. According to the second interpretation, on the other hand, logical structures result from the progressive equilibration of the prelogical structures which are the prototype of the later structures. Equilibration would thus explain the process of transition from the prelogical to the logical mathematical structure and, hence, the formation and above all the completion of these structures.

Many years of research have shown not that there is logic everywhere, which would be absurd (the first "concrete operations" having to do with classes, relations, and numbers appear only at the age of seven to eight, while the propositional or formal operations appear only at about the age of eleven to twelve), but that at all age levels structures exist which are the prototypes of logic and which by progressive equilibration lead to logico-mathematical structures. Infantile sensorimotor schemata, for example, herald later classifications, relational judgments, and inferences (transitivity, etc.). Likewise, in perception one also discerns prototypical structures (witness the return to Helmholtz manifested in the "new look" of Bruner and Postman [1949] in transaction theory, etc.).

At our Center of Genetic Epistemology in Geneva we have been investigating the question of whether there is a definite and stable dividing line between observation and inference. We never have a pure observation which antedated any logical or prelogical structure. When children of different developmental levels are presented with two parallel rows of unequal length each consisting of four discs with or without traits linking the elements with one' another, the perception of the equality of the two collections (when presented rapidly) varies according to the level of development. Depending upon whether or not the subject already has a schema of correspondence and the extent to which it is elaborated, perception is modified because of "preinferences" analogous to those described by Helmholtz. The problem of distinguishing what is given from the inferential elements permitting their interpretation extends to perception and the mechanisms inherent in it [Piaget and Morf, 1958].

In short, logical structures are anticipated by weaker prototypic structures which are partially isomorphic to them. Truly logical structures are distinguished by their complete reversibility, i.e., by the presence of direct and inverse operations that exactly compensate one another and thus effect a permanent equilibrium. What characterizes logical structures genetically is the fact that they evolve from more primitive structures which are only semireversible, i.e., only semiequilibrated and only partially compensated. These semirevers le structures which herald the logical structures are the set of sensorimotor retroactions and anticipations, the set of regulatory processes whose progressive forms of compensation assure a gradual equilibration resulting finally in logical reversibility. In this manner, the feedbacks or reafferences already constitute processes of equilibration whose compensations prefigure reversibility. The anticipations which result from these retroactions for their part prepare operational mobility, and the union of retroactions and anticipations provides a sketch of what the reversible operations will become when the compensations are both complete and permanent.

In conclusion, the development of cognitive functions is characterized by a succession of stages. Only the last stages (seven to eight and eleven to twelve years) mark the completion of the operational or logical structures, but even the earliest stages are oriented in this direction. The development of cognitive functions consists, above all, of a process of equilibration. The difference between the prelogical and logical structures depends essentially on the partial or complete character of the compensations involved, hence on the degree of reversibility attained by the structures. We refer to degree of reversibility since reversibility does not depend on an all-or-nothing law; it involves an infinite number of degrees from the most elementary to the highest regulations.

It is no exaggeration to speak of the central explanatory role played by the concept of equilibrium in questions concerning the development of cognitive functions. However, there remains the whole problem of explaining the process of transition from the relatively unequilibrated or unstable sensorimotor and perceptual structures to the highly equilibrated structures of logical operations. This problem leads us to the examination of equilibrium itself.

2. MODELS OF EQUILIBRIUM

Models of equilibrium are to be found in mechanics, in thermodynamics, in physical chemistry, in biology, in econometrics, etc., and all kinds of terms have been used with respect to them. We shall consider only those three models that have been applied or are applicable to psychology.

The first model is that of field forces whose equilibrium is defined by an exact balance of forces (the algebraic sum of vector forces being zero). Gestalt studies of perception and intelligence are of this kind. However, this model raises objections from biology: homeostasis does not, in fact, involve exact balances but is frequently overbalanced because of protective and cautious responses to intrusion. The same holds *a fortiori* for the perceptual field: the situation suggested by the facts is not that of a precise balance but of a protection against error. Thus, perceptual constancies, which should be the model of rigorous "balances," demonstrate instead remarkable overcompensations. For example, size constancy (which we have been studying from a genetic point of view with Lambercier,[3] using a variety of techniques) usually appears in young children as a systematic underconstancy, whereas with older children and adults one usually observes a systematic overconstancy. Near perfect constancy is found only, on the average, at around nine to ten years.

In connection with the higher cognitive functions, the model of balanced forces is even more inadequate because of the redundancies utilized by logic. If the perceptual overconstancies testify to an attitude of precaution against error, logic in its entirety may be considered, from the point of view of information theory, as a system of precorrections for anticipated errors, as demonstrated by L. Apostel [1957] at our Center. This entails a set of anticipatory activities whose reversibility (the structure of the "group," etc.) is inherent in them. Thus, with respect to logic, one cannot speak of a balance of forces in an actual or static sense but only of a system of compensations related to the operations themselves.

A second model of equilibrium is the probabilistic model utilized, for example, by Ashby [1947] in his enlightening study on cerebral dynamics. There are processes of neural equilibration manifested by the habituation of small compensations and by new adaptations to more complex stimuli. Ashby explains them by an indefinitely increasing probability in a commutative system, represented here by the organism and its environment. Such a model should be retained by psychology but translated into terms of differentiated activities.

The third model is that of equilibrium by compensation between external intrusion and the activities of the subject. These activities could, for example, be described as strategies, as in the language of game theory. Such strategies have as their intention the diminution of losses and the augmentation of gains in information, either according to the usual criterion (Bayes theorem, 1763), or in minimizing the anticipated maximal losses (minima). Equilibrium thus corresponds to the saddle point of the matrix of imputation and by no means expresses a state of rest but a play of compensations involving a maximum amount of activity on the part of the subject.

This language of strategies must be translated into probabilistic terms. Each strategy must be characterized by an objective probability, so that in cases where the construction of the matrix of imputation is doubtful it is possible to confine oneself to the simple probabilistic description of successive reactions. This is what we shall do in the following examples.

We shall furnish one or two explicative examples of equilibrium in order to emphasize the fact that a cognitive equilibrium is always "mobile" (which in no way precludes its eventual stability) and in order to underline the fact that it always consists of a system of probable compensations of external intrusions by the activities of the subject. Our first example will be in the area of perception, because the perceptual structures are very unstable compared with logical structures, and hence they highlight the similarities and differences between the two levels of equilibria.

When a geometric optical illusion is exposed tachistoscopically at exposure times varying from .02 seconds to 1 second, it has been shown [Piaget, Bang, and Matalon, 1958] that the illusion, which is weak for very short exposures, usually reaches a maximum toward .1 to .5 seconds then slowly decreases toward a stable plateau. This maximum depends on the point of fixation (there is no maximum for certain fixation points), which can make an illusion either positive or negative. In Delboeuf's illusion, for example, adults seem to overestimate the width of the space between enclosed and enclosing circles at short exposures. Children, on the other hand, act as though they overestimate the enclosed circle itself, perhaps because they do not clearly differentiate it from the enclosing circle.

Now this temporal maximum—that must not be confused with the spatial maximum, which is dependent upon the proportions of the figure according to the law of relative centering which we have formulated elsewhere [Piaget, 1961]—is interesting from the point of view of perceptual equilibrium. It confirms the duality of the factors involved; on the one hand, the intrusions resulting from the characteristics of the figure and, on the other hand, the compensations resulting from the activities of the subject. If we assume that centering on a certain part of the figure corresponds to a set of "encounters" between parts of the figure and elements of the receptor organs, the apparent length of a particular side of the figure will be proportional to the number of such encounters. Hence there can be an absolute estimate which varies with the time of presentation.

We shall call the correspondence between the encounters on one of the sides and those which occur on another "couplings." The coupling will be complete if the encounters are homogeneous on the two sides. In this case, there will be no relative overestimation, whatever the absolute estimation. The coupling will be incomplete if the encounters are heterogeneous and, in this case, there will be relative overestimation of the favored side. As a general rule, the probability that the coupling will be complete—i.e., that the encounters will be homogeneous—is low. Hence there is a high probability of distortions or "illusions."

Two situations, however, augment the probability of complete couplings, hence of homogeneous encounters and the diminution of the illusion: (1) when the encounters are very infrequent, as is the case when the exposure times are very short, and (2) when the encounters are very frequent and tend toward saturation, as is the case with the detailed exploration of free vision or during long tachistoscopic presentations. If the increase in encounters is plotted against time in a logarithmic curve (not in a straight-line curve, since a point that has already been encountered adds nothing if the encounter is repeated), the estimates of the two sides will be expressed by two logarithmic curves with a common point of origin. The curves will be close together toward the outset and then depart farther and farther from each other and ultimately become joined anew in the course of long presentations. The temporal maximum thus corresponds to the maximum deviation between the two curves. For example, if one assigns a probability of .5 and .6 to the encounters of the two sides, there will theoretically be a temporal maximum for .2 and .3 seconds, which corresponds to the actual times we have observed.

In such a case, the equilibrium (which naturally does not correspond to the maximum that remains unstable but to the final plateau where the two logarithmic curves present a slight, relatively constant, deviation corresponding to the average illusion in free vision) is due to a system of compensations between the intrusions of the figure (counteracting the homogeneity of the encounters and translated in the form of distortions owing to centering) and an activity of the subject in the direction of complete coupling (decentering) through homogenization of the encounters. This process can be described in terms of perceptual strategies which consist of choosing the best points of centering in order to minimize the distortions owing to incomplete couplings, i.e., of heterogeneous encounters. Here is proof enough that after n repetitions the adult may reach the stage of null illusions. Perceptual equilibrium, even though unstable, is thus gained through the activities of the subject which tend to compensate the distorting influence of the stimulus.

Another example of cognitive equilibrium which can be explained analogously is that of processes leading to concepts of conservation, such as, for example, the conservation of matter when a ball of clay is transformed into a sausage. The most probable strategy at the outset is concentration (representative rather than perceptual) on just one of the transformed characteristics.[4] For example, the quantity appears to increase because the object becomes elongated. Once this has occurred, the strategy which then becomes most probable consists of noticing the second transformed characteristic and supposing that the quantity diminishes because the sausage becomes thinner. Thereafter, a new strategy becomes most probable as a function of having attended to the two preceding characteristics (the second can be bypassed very rapidly). This new strategy consists of oscillating between these characteristics and vaguely noticing the interdependence of the sausage's elongation and its thinness. This third reaction leads to the accent's being placed on the transformation, by contrast with the static configurations alone. A fourth strategy ensues, which consists of the discovery of the compensations among the transformations and acceptance of the fact of conservation.

This example is illustrative of the progressive equilibration which leads to a logical or "necessary" structure. Apart from the first strategy, which has the greatest probability at the outset, each of the following strategies *becomes* the most probable one as a function of the preceding strategy. The succession of strategies thus occurs in a controlled sequence. Final equilibrium is thus the product of a compensation for the ambiguous stimuli by the activities of the subject, which in turn are characterized by successive probabilities.

It would be easy to give an analogous explanation of the discovery of operational methods of seriation, where the successive strategies are based on ascending and descending series and are finally fused in the operational system. The same explanation holds for the construction of inclusions, proper to the hierarchical classifications, which also involve a progressive synthesis of ascending $(A < B < C < \ldots)$ and descending

(C > B > A) relations. All this has already been discussed in our study on logic and equilibrium [Piaget, 1957].

3. CONCLUSION

Generally speaking, the equilibrium of cognitive structures can be conceived as a compensation for external intrusion by means of the activities of the subject, which are responses to these intrusions. The latter may be presented in two different ways.

In the case of the lower, unstable (sensorimotor and perceptual) forms of equilibrium, the intrusion consists of real and actual modifications of the environment, to which the compensatory activities of the subject respond as best they can without a permanent operational system. These are the forms of equilibrium described above apropos of the law of the temporal maximum of illusions.

In the case of the higher or operational structures, on the other hand, the intrusion to which the subject responds may consist of virtual modifications; i.e., in optimum cases they can be imagined and anticipated by the subject in the form of the direct operations of a system (operations expressing transformations in some initial sense). In this case, the compensatory activities will also consist of imagining and anticipating the transformations but in an inverse sense (reciprocal or inverse operations of a system of reversible operations).

In short, the compensations start by being effectuated by degrees but can end by consisting of pure representations of the transformations with the intrusions, like the compensations, being reduced to certain operations of the system. Between these two extremes there are, of course, all kinds of intervening steps, such as sensorimotor organizations (e.g., the schema of the permanent object), perceptual constancies, the induction of representative probabilities, etc.

In considering the operational (logico-mathematical) structures, i.e., the most equilibrated structures, we see that each constitutes the system of all possible transformations for a certain class of transformations, such as the classification group-ings or the combinatory groupings of propositional logic, etc. Then we see that certain transformations can be envisaged as modifications of the system owing to intrusions. The inverse transformations will thus consist of virtual compensations of these original transformations. The operational system is thus comparable to a system of vector forces in physics whose alge-braic sum is zero. But in physics the vector forces are, by definition, not "real," since they exist only in the mind of the physicist. In the case of the operational system, by contrast, the virtual transformations exist in the mind of the subject. The mind is the proper domain of psychology, so that the virtual transformations correspond to the subject's real operations. This is why the concept of equilibrium is explicative in psychol-ogy.

In short, the stable and final psychological equilibrium of the cognitive structures is confounded with the reversibility of the operations, since the inverse operations exactly compensate the direct transformations. But this poses a final problem. Is it the reversibility of the operations that engenders their equilib-rium or is it the progressive equilibration of the actions—passing through the stages of simple regulations with their retroactions and anticipations—which ends by engendering their terminal reversibility? Here the results of genetic analysis seem decisive. Since the "compensations" which respond to the intrusion ad-just themselves only progressively and at first incompletely, the operational reversibility expressed by the complete compensa-tions must be the result and not the cause of gradual equilibra-tion. This, however, does not prevent the operational structures, once constituted, from acceding to the rank of instruments or organs for subsequent equilibration.

NOTES

[1] Originally published in *Acta Psychologica*, 1954, X, 51–60.

[2] A ludic symbol is one related to or derived from play activity. Ed.

[3] A footprint, for example, is an index of the animal who made it. A signal, on the other hand, is a stimulus which occurs with the object but is not causally related to it. The bell associated with food presentation in classical conditioning is a good example of a neutral stimulus which comes to be a signal. Ed.

[4] This is a somewhat confused and confusing example. A more clear-cut illustration is as follows:

obs. 64 At 1;7 (20) Jacqueline watches me when I put a coin in my hand and then put my hand under a coverlet. I withdraw my hand closed; Jacqueline opens it, then searches under the coverlet until she finds the object. [Piaget, 1954.]

In this example the transitivity relation is clear: the coin was in the hand; the hand was under the coverlet; therefore the coin is under the coverlet. Ed.

CHAPTER 5

Problems of Genetic Psychology [1]

⧉ THE OBJECT OF this study is not only to communicate some of the recent results of our research but also to indicate the spirit in which it was undertaken. We have studied the development of intelligence for over thirty years and the development of perception as a function of age for over ten years. I should like to describe our objectives in undertaking this work.

Studies of child psychology can, of course, be undertaken in order to understand the child himself better or in order to perfect pedagogical methods. These goals, however, are common to all work in genetic psychology, so we shall not dwell on them. Our objective—in addition to the aforementioned aims —is even more ambitious. We believe that all research in scientific psychology must start from principles of development and that the formation of mental mechanisms in the child best explains their nature and functioning in the adult. It seems to us that the essential goal of child psychology is to construct an expository method for scientific psychology in general; in other words, to furnish the indispensable genetic dimension to the solution of all mental problems. In the field of intelligence, for example, it is impossible to furnish an exact psychological interpretation of the logical operations, the concepts of number, space, time, etc., without previously studying the development of these operations and concepts. This, of course, includes social development in the form of the growth of societies and the diverse collective forms of thought, especially scientific thought, and also individual development. There is nothing contradictory in this, since the development of the child consists in, among other things, the progressive socialization of the individual. In the field of perception it would be impossible to construct an exact theory of perceptual "constancies," of geometric illusions, or of the structuring of perceptual space according to horizontal and vertical coordinates, etc., without previously studying the development of these phenomena, if only in order to guard against too facile hypotheses concerning what is innate.

1. INNATENESS AND ACQUISITION

To determine the possible role of nature and nurture (either of physical experience or of social influence) in the determination of behavior, we must study the genetic formation of the behavior in question. It has, for example, frequently been claimed that the child has an "instinct of imitation." Now the study of the development of imitation from four to six months and eighteen to twenty-four months allows us to follow, step by step, the true learning this function requires and the relationship between the learning of imitation and the developing sensorimotor intelligence. The "errors" of imitation that occur are highly significant. For example, one of my children, in the presence of a model which consisted of opening and closing the eyes, began responding by opening and closing his mouth [Piaget, 1951(d)]!

Moreover, recourse to innate factors never resolves problems; it merely passes them on to biology, and as long as the fundamental question of the inheritance of acquired characteristics is not definitively resolved, it may always be supposed that modifications resulting from environmental influence will be found at the origin of an innate mechanism. Personally, we have always thought it impossible to explain innate sensorimotor behaviors without this hypothesis of the inheritance of acquired characteristics, and this is particularly so in the case of the (absolute) reflexes which are the most important sensorimotor reactions of the first year [Piaget, 1952(c)]. In order to form an opinion on this essential question, a few years ago, having studied the zoology of mollusks before studying child psychology, we analyzed the sensorimotor adaptations of the *Limnaea Stagnalis*, which, appearances notwithstanding, has a direct bearing on developmental psychology. The *Limnaea Stagnalis* is a freshwater mollusk which has an elongated shape in the marshes, but in the large lakes with smooth and pebbly banks it takes on a contracted and globular shape because of the movements the animal makes during its growth in order to resist the agitation of the water. In studying the heredity of these contracted lake *Limnaea* in the aquarium, using pure and cross breeding, we were able to establish that this shape is not a simple phenotype but is inherited with stability over six to seven generations [Piaget, 1929(a); 1929(b)]. The mutationists, of course, told us that this was merely a fortuitous mutation that had survived in the lakes but was eliminated for some reason in the marsh waters. However, what is interesting is that while the elongated form cannot live in lakes or in pebbly places exposed to waves, the contracted form can live anywhere. We transplanted it twenty-seven years ago to a marsh, where its descendants are still prospering and have conserved the lake shape. It is thus very difficult to explain by chance alone the formation of this race, adapted to the movements of the water, which is observed only on the most exposed banks of large lakes! We see no explanation possible in this instance other than the intervention of environmental action on the reflex mechanism and on morphogenesis.

Reverting to the child—if one were led to concede certain innate elements, for example in the perception of space (this cannot be excluded, even though not proved with respect to the three dimensions, for we cannot imagine but can only conceive space with four or *n* dimensions), there remains the question of whether we are dealing with heredity of endogenous origin or heredity stemming from ancestral acquisitions as a function of the environment and of experience.

This dual possibility is particularly applicable to a factor whose importance has certainly been exaggerated in child psychology even though it plays an undeniable role in it. This is the maturation of the nervous system, on which Gesell [1945] founded all his work and Wallon [1945] a part of his. Two remarks are important in this respect, in addition to those we have already made with respect to the inheritance of acquired characteristics.

The first is that maturation is undoubtedly never independent of a certain functional exercise where experience plays a role. For example, since Tournay's [1934] research, it has been generally conceded that the coordination between vision and prehension is effectuated at around four and a half months (myelinization of the pyramidal fissure). Now in the case of my three (full-term) children, the three concomitant signs of this coordination (grabbing an object in the visual field, grabbing an object outside the visual field and bringing it in front of the eyes) were manifested in one at six months, the second at four and a half months, and the third at three months, without there being any notable difference in intellectual level among them [Piaget, 1952(c)]. The first child had been the object of few experiments, whereas with the third I had made a series of experiments, as of the age of two months, on the imitation of hand movements. Exercise thus appears to play a role in the acceleration or retardation of certain forms of maturation.

The second remark is that the maturation of the nervous system simply opens up a series of possibilities (and nonmaturation involves a series of impossibilities), but without giving rise to an immediate actualization of these possibilities so long as the conditions of material experience or social interaction do not bring about this actualization. One could, for example, ask whether the logical operations are innate. More than thirty years of study of the subject has led us to consider this as extremely unlikely. One of the arguments which could be invoked in favor of innateness would be that the neural connections themselves present a certain structure isomorphic to logic. The neurological law of all-or-nothing can in fact be translated into a binary arithmetic (one and/o) isomorphic to Booleian algebra [Boole, 1854]. McCulloch and Pitts [1943] have shown that neural connections take the form of the diverse operations of the logic of propositional functions (dysjunction, conjunction, exclusion, etc.). While we freely admit that these facts constitute a necessary condition for the formation of logic, we do not feel that they are a sufficient condition, because the logical structures become constituted only little by little in the course of the child's development. They are constructed gradually in connection with language and, above all, in connection with social exchange. The neural system, with its late maturation (myelogenesis and, above all, cytodendrogenesis), is thus confined to opening a few of the possibilities from which a certain number of behaviors will be actualized (and no doubt relatively few in proportion to the number of possibilities that remain open). This actualization presupposes certain conditions of physical experience such as the manipulation of objects, etc., which is also essential for logic, and certain social conditions such as the regulated exchange of information, mutual control, etc. It is these diverse conditions that determine the completion of what would be impossible through maturation alone.

2. THE PROBLEM OF THE NECESSITY
PROPER TO THE LOGICAL STRUCTURES

If logic is not innate in the child, there remains a difficult problem for general psychology to solve: it is the problem of how logical necessity emerges in the child. For example, if $A = B$ and if $B = C$, the small child is by no means certain that $A = C$ (we shall give examples of this later), whereas after seven or eight years and, above all, at eleven to twelve years, it is impossible for him not to conclude that A = C.

Logic in the child (as in the adult) is evidenced in the form of operational structures; i.e., the logical act consists essentially of *operating*, hence of acting on things and toward people. An operation is, in effect, an internalized action which has become *reversible* and coordinated with other operations in a grouping, governed by the laws of the system as a whole. To say that *an operation is reversible* is to say that every operation corresponds to an inverse operation, as is true, for example, for logical or arithmetic addition and subtraction. An operation never exists in isolation. It is dependent on an operational structure such as the "groups" in mathematics (direct operation $+1$, inverse operation -1, identical operation $1 - 1 = 0$, and associative operation $[1 + 1] - 1 = 1 + [1 - 1]$), or lattices (studied by the great Russian mathematician Glivenko under the name of "structures"), or the structures that are more elementary than groups and networks, which we call "groupings" [Piaget, 1950]. Each of these structures involves laws of totalities which define the operational system as such and a particular form of reversibility (inversion in the group, reciprocity in the lattice, etc.).

The psychological criterion of operational structures and in consequence of complete reversibility (a characteristic that emerges gradually in the course of development) is the elaboration of invariants or concepts of conservation. For example, at what we shall call the level of preoperational representation, children of four to six years, after they themselves have filled two small glasses with equal quantities of beads (by putting a blue bead in the left-hand glass with one hand while putting a red bead in the right-hand glass with the other hand), think that the quantities are no longer equal if they empty one of these glasses into a different container that is narrower and higher. They think that the quantity of beads is not conserved in the course of this transfer. By contrast, with the formation of the first concrete operational structures at the age of seven to eight, the child argues that the quantity must be conserved (once again the feeling of necessity) because the beads have merely been displaced and can be put back again as they were before (reversibility), [Piaget, 1952(a)]. The construction of this concept of conservation is thus typical of a certain operational level.

With the aid of these criteria, which we did not invent *a priori* but discovered empirically, four main stages can be distinguished in the development of logic in the child:

1) From birth to one and a half to two years, one can speak of a sensorimotor period prior to language where there are neither operations, properly speaking, nor logic but where actions are already organized according to certain structures which herald or prepare for reversibility and the construction of invariants. For example, at around five to six months, the baby evidences no searching behavior when an object has disappeared from his visual field (he does not lift up a handkerchief placed over a toy he had intended to grab, etc.), whereas at around twelve to eighteen months, the object has become permanent and gives rise to systematic searching behavior as a function of its successive positions. The construction of this first invariant—the permanent object in proximal space—is linked to an organization of the subject's own movements and the displacements of the object according to what geometrists call the "group of displacements." Here there is a remarkable beginning of practical reversibility [Piaget, 1954].

2) Between two and seven to eight years of age one finds the first union of thought with language, as well as the first intimations of symbolic play, deferred imitation, mental imagery, and other forms of the symbolic function. This increasing representation results largely from a progressive internalization of actions which had heretofore actually been performed on the sensorimotor plane. Internalized actions, however, by no means reach the level of reversible operations, because on the plane of representation it is much more difficult than it seems to invert actions. It is, for example, much more difficult to represent, on

the road back from a given destination, the order of landmarks just enumerated on the way out. Without the reversible operations and the groupings to which they give rise, the child cannot grasp the conservation of discontinuous quantities (say, a set of beads) or of continuous quantities (say, an amount of liquid) when their perceptual dimensions are transformed by placing them in a tall narrow container after they were first perceived in a wide shallow container. We have just given an example of this with respect to discontinuous quantities (the beads in the glass receptacle). Here is another example with respect to continuous quantities. The child is given two balls of modeling clay of the same dimensions and weight, then one ball is transformed into a cake, a sausage, etc. The child is then asked (a) if the balls still contain the same amount of clay, (b) if they are the same weight, and (c) if the volume is still the same. (For the volume experiment, the ball of clay is immersed in a glass of water and the subject is asked whether the cake or the sausage, etc., "will take up as much space" in another glass of water.) An understanding of the conservation of the quantity of matter is acquired only at about seven to eight years, on the average, that of weight at around nine to ten years, and that of volume at around the age of eleven to twelve [Piaget and Inhelder, 1941]. Comparable experiments with length, distance, and area reveal that these quantities are conserved only at about the age of seven to eight [Piaget and Inhelder, 1956].

In areas not yet structured by concepts of conservation, the other elementary logical links that derive from the use of operations, such as transitivity, commutativity, etc., are also not yet observed. With respect to transitivity, for example, a child can be given two identical brass bars so that he notices the equality of their weights, i.e., that A = B. He then is asked to compare the weight of B with that of a lead ball C. The child expects that C will be heavier, but he notices on the scale that B = C. Finally he is asked whether or not A = C, after being reminded of the equalities A = B and B = C. At the preoperational level which, in the case of weight, lasts until around eight to nine years, the child is convinced that the lead ball C will be heavier than A in spite of the previously noted equalities. Some subjects have even told us: "It's all very well for them to be equal once $(A = C)$, but this time the lead ball will be heavier $(C > A)$, because it is heavier" [Piaget and Inhelder, 1941].

3) At around seven to eight years, on the average (needless to say, these average ages are dependent on the social and educational environment), the child—after interesting transition phases whose details we shall not discuss here—arrives at the constitution of a logic and of operational structures which we shall call "concrete." This "concrete" stage, as opposed to formal characteristics of true logic, is particularly instructive for the psychology of logical operations in general. It signifies that at this level, the level of the beginnings of logic proper, the operations are not as yet concerned with propositions or verbal declarations but with objects themselves and are confined to classifying, seriating, putting in correspondence with one another, etc. In other words, the nascent operation is still linked with manipulative action that is barely ideational.

Nonetheless, however close they remain to action, these "concrete operations" are already organized into reversible structures which present their laws of totality. There are, for example, classifications. In effect, a logical class does not exist in an isolated state but only to the extent that it is linked by diverse inclusions with the general system of hierarchical nestings which constitute a system of classification. Thus the direct operation is the addition of classes $(A + A' = B)$ and the inverse operation is the subtraction of classes based on reversibility by inversion or negation $(B - A' = A$ or $A - A = o)$. Another essential concrete structure is seriation, which consists of ordering objects according to an increasing or decreasing property $(A < B < C < . . .)$. Its reversibility consists of reciprocity, as is the case in all structures of relations. The multiplicative structures (correspondences, matrices, etc.) also appear at this concrete operational stage [Piaget and Inhelder, 1959].[3]

In short, the first concrete structures are all based on the operations of classes and relations (but without exhausting either the logic of classes or that of relations) and become organized according to easily defined laws. We have called these structures, whose most direct psychological consequence is the construction of concepts of conservation, "elementary groupings," in contrast to the logical groups and lattices of a higher level. Their essential function consists of systematically organizing the various areas of experience, but they do not as yet completely differentiate between content and form. For example, the same operations are employed with respect to the quantity of matter, to weight, and to volume, but they are applied to matter one or two years before weight and to weight one or two years before volume.

4) Finally, at around eleven to twelve years new operations appear by means of the progressive generalization of preceding operations and become stabilized at around fourteen to fifteen years. These are the operations of "logical propositions," which, from this time on, can deal with simple verbal statements (propositions), i.e., with simple hypotheses rather than exclusively with objects. Hypothetico-deductive reasoning thus becomes possible and with it the constitution of a "formal" logic, i.e., a logic applicable to any kind of content.

Two new groupings are formed at this stage which mark the completion of the uncompleted structures of the previous level. These are:

A. The "lattice" of propositional logic manifested by the appearance of combinatory operations. It is remarkable to see the ability of a preadolescent of eleven to twelve years (this age is always relative to the subject's social milieu) to find—without formal education in this regard (at least in Geneva)—systematic methods for grouping objects according to all the combinations from 1 to n (as far as n = 3, 4, or 5). For example, in an experiment of B. Inhelder's [Inhelder and Piaget, 1958] the subject is given four jars containing colorless and odorless liquids. When a few drops of reagent are added, two of the liquids turn yellow, a third is neutral, and the fourth contains a decoloring agent. The task is simply to reproduce the color yellow. Subjects of eleven to twelve years proceed with this task with a combinatory system unknown up to this point. The propositional operations constituted at the same level are also based on a combinatory system. It is thus difficult to conceive that it is by chance alone that the capacity to combine objects or propositions is constituted at the same age and in all areas, while at the level of concrete operations there was only a system of simple nesting. From the mathematical point of view, this may be expressed by saying that the simple sets are superseded by "the set of all subsets," which is a lattice that simultaneously establishes the combinatory operations and those of propositional logic.

B. Closely correlated with the structure of lattices, a "group" structure of four transformations (Klein's group) is formed. This is also of great importance to the reasoning characteristic of adolescence. Let us take a propositional operation such as "either p or q or both," which is symbolized by $p \vee q$. Let us call the identical transformation which leaves $p \vee q$ unchanged, I. The operation can be negated so that if N is the inversion or negation: $N (p \vee q) = \bar{p} . \bar{q}$ ("neither p nor q"). The reciprocal R of $p \vee q$, which is $\bar{p} \vee \bar{q}$ (either non-p or non-q), and its correlative C, which is $p . q$ ("both p and q"), can also be established. We then have the commutative group $NR = C$; $NC = R$; $CR = N$; and $NRC = I$.

This structure is involved both in the verbal reasoning of the adolescent and in much experimental reasoning that is transformed by this capacity for formal thought. For example, in reasoning about a system in mechanical or hydrostatic equilibrium, there is the action $= I$, its negation $= N$, the reaction $= R$, and its negation $= C$. If there are two conjoined systems of reference—for example, the movement of a snail on a plank being displaced at the same time—for one of the systems, there are the transformations I and N and for the other the transformations R and C with all the combinations among them. This structure plays its most general role, however, in the acquisition of the operational schemata of the mathematical proportions, since for an operation x there is the logical proportion $Ix/Rx = Cx/Nx$. At this same age the concept of proportions becomes comprehensible to the child [Inhelder and Piaget, 1958].

How can we explain the child's progressive transition from an astonishing insensibility to the most simple deductions to the specific state of awareness which characterizes logical necessity (if p is true [e.g., $A = B$ and $B = C$] then q is necessarily true $[A = C]$)? Four distinct factors may be considered: the innateness of the structures in the nervous system, physical experience, social transmission, and the probabilistic laws of equilibrium.

We have already said enough about the factor of innateness. Let us simply recall that while the coordinations of the nervous system determine the framework of possibilities and impossibilities within which the logical structures will be constructed, these logical structures do not exist within the nervous system as embryonic instruments of thought. An entire construction is necessary in order to lead from the nervous system to logic, so logic cannot be considered innate.

Should logical necessity be conceived as drawn from physical experience with logical rules constituting the most universal laws applicable to objects themselves ("the physics of the commonplace object" to which Gonseth [1936] refers)? Certainly it is only when actions are exercised upon objects that the logical structures are formed. We have emphasized the fact that the source of logical operations is action itself, which, of course, takes place only in connection with objects. In addition, the stage of "concrete operations" shows that, before it is applied to pure verbal statements or "propositions," logic is organized in the midst of practical manipulations bearing upon objects. Finally, it goes without saying that the physical laws pertaining to objects conform to the rules of conservation (or identity), transitivity, commutativity, etc., as well as to the operations of addition (plus its inverse, dissociation or subtraction) and multiplication (plus its inverse, logical abstraction: if $A \times B = AB$, then $AB : A = B$). In other words, physical laws conform to the most universal logical structures.

A fundamental factor must be taken into account. This is that objects are constantly changed through action and that these transformations constitute new sources of knowledge. One of Karl Marx's primary sociological propositions is that man acts on nature in order to be productive but at the same time is conditioned by the laws of nature. This interaction between the properties of the object and the properties of human productivity is found also in the psychology of knowledge. We can get to know objects only by acting on them and by producing some transformation in them. For example, the logical operations of classifying or seriating consist of "producing" collections or a certain order of succession by means of the properties of the objects employed.

With this in mind, the development of logical necessity becomes understandable, whereas it would remain inexplicable if it consisted merely of noting the properties of the object. For example, the "identical operation" $\pm o$ (which boils down to an addition or subtraction of the null class o) of necessity results from the composition between the direct operation $+A$ and the inverse operation $-A$, so that $+A - A = \pm o$. This signifies that to add a set and then to take it away is equivalent to neither adding nor subtracting. The feeling of necessity which goes along with this conclusion does not stem from merely noting the properties of the objects of collection A, which would give rise to a pure statement of fact and not to an awareness of necessity; it results from the coordination of the actions of adding and subtracting in the production of the classification.

While action is involved in the structuring of the logical operations, the social factor in the constitution of these structures must also be taken into account, for the individual is always socialized to some extent. For example, the necessity inherent in the principle of contradiction presents all the characteristics—in addition to those related to the coordination of actions—of a true collective obligation, since it is, above all, with respect to others that we are obliged not to contradict ourselves. If some day we say the opposite of what we have said the previous day, it would be easy to forget the contradiction if our social partners did not oblige us to make a choice and to remain faithful to the statements we have chosen!

Distinctions among the various possible types of social relationships must be introduced because they do not all lead to logic. Logical rules are not imposed by the social group like rules of grammar, such as the agreement of the verb with its subject, etc., i.e., by the simple authority of usage and common consent. The form of collective interaction which intervenes in the constitution of the logical structures is essentially the coordination of interpersonal actions through common work and verbal exchange. When this collective coordination of actions is analyzed, it can be seen that the coordination consists of operations but that these are interpersonal rather than intraindividual. For example, what one person does is completed by another (addition) or corresponds with what is being done by others (multiplicative correspondence). Similarly, what one person does may differ from what is being done by others, but these different points of view can be interrelated (reciprocity), etc. On the other hand, arguments and disagreements give rise to negations and inverse operations, etc. In short, there are not intraindividual coordinations of actions on the one hand and the social life which unifies them on the other. There is a fundamental identity between the interpersonal operations and the intraindividual operations so that they can be isolated only by abstraction from a totality where the biological and social factors of action constantly interact with one another [Piaget, 1950].

A fourth factor must be mentioned which is too often forgotten but whose importance will undoubtedly be shown increasingly in future research. This is the factor of equilibrium linked to probabilistic considerations. First of all, it is apparent that each of the preceding three factors is subject to laws of equilibrium and that their interaction involves a form of equilibration. The coordination of the actions of an individual subject is manifested through momentary disequilibria (corresponding to needs or problems) and through re-equilibrations (corresponding to satisfactions or solutions). It goes without saying that the social coordination of actions involves both disequilibria and forms of equilibrium and that the interactions among the personal (neurological, etc.) factors and the social factors of action stem from a continual equilibration. But the notion of equilibrium has a much more precise meaning in the psychology of logical operations than it does in other fields. We have seen that an operation is essentially a reversible action, since for any given operation (such as $+A$ or $+1$) there is always its corresponding inverse ($-A$ or -1). It is this reversibility which enables the child to understand the conservation of a quantity or of a set when its spatial disposition is altered, since when the modification is seen as reversible, it follows that the quantity in question remains invariant. Reversibility develops progressively in the course of the child's mental evolution. The child at the sensorimotor level is aware only of a practical reversibility in proximal space (the "group of displacements" built up during the second year of life) and the preoperational representations only present a semireversibility on the plane of thought linked to approximate regulations or compensations (correction of a gross error, etc.). The concrete operations comprise two parallel forms of reversibility, inversion or negation in the operations of classes and reciprocity in the operations of relations. Finally, at the level of the formal operations, the INRC group fuses these two forms of reversibility into a single system through the establishment of inversions and reciprocities. This growing reversibility assures progress toward equilibrium, since physical equilibrium is defined by its reversibility. A system is in equilibrium when all the virtual transformations (equivalent here to possible operations) are compensated, i.e., when for each possible transformation there is a corresponding possible transformation of equal value, oriented in the opposite direction.

Whether we say that the operations are organized into reversible structures or that they tend toward certain forms of equilibrium thus amounts to the same thing.

This progress toward equilibrium is of great theoretical importance, since it may be possible some day to provide a calculus based on probabilistic considerations. If one thinks, for example, of the second principle of thermodynamics and how easily it is explained by the calculation of probabilities, it becomes apparent how important a factor equilibrium is in explaining the formation of logical structures and logical necessity.

3. THE DEVELOPMENT OF PERCEPTION

These probabilistic considerations can easily be applied to the study of the development of perception. We have already arrived at some relatively precise schemata and formulae to explain some well-known phenomena and, on occasion, to anticipate certain new phenomena.

The genetic study of perception, and particularly of perceptual "illusions," is especially instructive, since it allows for the distribution of perceptual phenomena—which are highly complex and still poorly understood, in spite of the efforts of scientific psychology for over a century—into different categories of distinctly different significance based on their development with age.

Perceptual illusions develop in at least three different ways. There are those which remain relatively constant or diminish in importance with age (for example, the illusions of angles, of Müller-Lyer, of Delboeuf, etc.); those which increase in importance with age (for example, the overestimation of the vertical as compared with the horizontal); and those which increase up to a certain level, in general nine to eleven years, only to diminish shortly thereafter (for example, the illusion of weight, the comparison of obliques, etc.). Whereas the two last categories, which are fairly closely related, constitute the aftereffects of diverse perceptual or sensorimotor activities in which movements of looking, establishing relationships with referents at a distance, etc., intervene, the illusions of the first category derive from more "primary" effects, i.e., from an approximately simultaneous interaction of all the elements perceived in the same field. We shall start with the first category.

Instead of contenting ourselves with a "Gestalt" interpretation, which provides a good description but is by no means explanatory, we have tried, on the one hand, to reduce the set of primary illusions (at any rate, the illusions of geometric planes) to one quantitative law and, on the other hand, to explain this law in terms of probability theory.

This law does not, of course, seek to determine the absolute value of the illusions, because the value diminishes on the average with age and varies widely from one individual to another. Given the diverse illusions which can be produced by varying the dimensions or the proportions of a figure, what it does seek to do is to determine the shape of the error curve as a function of these transformations. It seeks especially to determine which proportions of the figure will produce the maximum positive and negative illusions and the median null illusion (the intermediary point between positive and negative illusions).

Take, for example [Piaget and Denis-Prinzhorn, 1953], a rectangle of which one side A remains constant at 5 cm. and the other side A' is varied. Experimental measures show not only that when A > A', side A is overestimated and side A' is underestimated (at all ages), but also that the maximum positive illusion occurs when A' is as small as possible, in other words when the rectangle is reduced to a straight line. When A' = A (a square), there is a median null illusion. When A' is greater than A, A' is overestimated, but this is not the case indefinitely, and if A' is increased further, the curve of negative illusions is no longer a straight line but becomes an equilateral hyperbole tending toward an asymptote.

The experimental curve that is generated has the same shape

at all ages, but since error diminishes with age, the curve flattens without losing its qualitative characteristics. The same is true—but with very differently shaped curves—of many other illusions we have studied in subjects from the age of five or six to adulthood, such as the Delboeuf illusion (concentric circles), of angles, of the median of angles, of the Oppel-Kundt (divided spaces), of curves, of the Müller-Lyer, etc.

It is interesting to note that all the curves obtained can be subsumed under a single law, which is variously interpreted according to the figures and permits the construction in each case of a theoretical curve which so far has corresponded satisfactorily enough with the respective experimental curves. We shall discuss this law in a few words simply in order to give some general idea of it, but our main goal here is to show how the law can be explained in probabilistic terms.

Let L_1 = the greater of two comparative lengths of a figure (for example, the larger side of a rectangle) and L_2 = the smaller of the two lengths (for example, the smaller side of a rectangle). Let Lmax = the greatest length of the figure (in the case of a rectangle Lmax = L_1, but if L_1 and L_2 are two straight lines which are continuous then Lmax = $L_1 + L_2$, etc.). Let L = the length chosen as unity and on which the measurement will be made (in the case of a rectangle, $L = L_1$ or L_2, depending on the figure). Let n be the number of comparisons $(L_1 - L_2)$ which interact in the figure and let S = the surface. Let P = the illusion.

The law can then be expressed as follows:

$$P = \pm\frac{(L_1 - L_2)L_2 \times (nL{:}Lmax)}{S} = \frac{nL(L_1 - L_2)L_2}{S \cdot Lmax}$$

For example, in the case of rectangles, with A constant and A′ variable, if $A > A'$ (or $L = A$ and $n = \frac{A}{A} = 1$):

$$P = +\frac{(A - A')A' \times (A{:}A)}{AA'} = \frac{A - A'}{A}$$

With A constant and A' variable, if $A' > A$ (or $L = A$ and $n = \dfrac{A'}{A}$):

$$P = -\frac{(A' - A)A \times (A':A')}{AA'} = \frac{A' - A}{A'}$$

The simplicity of this law is thus apparent, since it reduces to a difference multiplied by the term $(L_1 - L_2)\ L_2$, a relationship $(nL:Lmax)$, and a product (S).

We have called this formula the "law of relative centrations." It is readily explainable in probabilistic terms that take into account both Weber's law and the fact that the effects deriving from these mechanisms diminish with age.

Let us hypothesize that every element on which vision is focused is overestimated. This "effect of centration" can be shown tachistoscopically. If the subject fixates on a segment in front of him and compares it with another segment at the periphery, the fixated or centered segment is overestimated. This is a highly complex phenomenon, since, in addition to the topographical factors, there are such additional intervening factors as attention, distinctness, order and duration of presentation, etc., as well as the technical factors of distance between the subject and the image being presented, of angles, etc.

Whether this overestimation by centration derives physiologically from the irradiation of stimulated neural cells, which is probable, or whether it derives from other factors, such as the small oscillating movements of the eyeball, which no doubt play a role in the visual exploration of the figure, it is not difficult to formulate a corresponding probabilistic schema which has both physiological and psychological significance.

Let us take a simple straight line of 4 to 5 cm. and mentally cut it up into a certain number of equal segments so that, for example, $N = 1000$. Furthermore, let us assume that there is a certain number of elements—whether on the retina, in the transmission organs, or in the visual cortex—which must encounter at least a part of these thousand segments in order for the line to be perceived. Suppose, for example, that an initial group of these neural elements encounters BN segments, where B is a constant fraction during an initial time period t. There will then remain N_1 segments not yet encountered, so that:

$$N_1 = (N - NB) = N(1 - B)$$

After the second n encounters, N_2 segments will remain which have not yet been encountered:

$$N_2 = (N_1 - N_1B) = N(1 - B)^2$$

After the third n encounters, there will remain N_3 segments which have not yet been encountered:

$$N_3 = (N_2 - N_2B) = N(1 - B)^3 \ldots \text{etc.}$$

The sum of segments encountered will equal NB, then $(NB + N_1B)$, then $(NB + N_1B + N_2B)$, etc. These sums thus furnish the model for what could be progressive (momentary or relatively enduring) overestimation due to centering on a line perceived during periods n, 2n, 3n, etc., or with increasing intensity or distinctness, etc. It is obvious that this model is subject to a logarithmic law, since the arithmetic progression n, 2n, 3n, etc., corresponds to the geometric progression $(1 - B)$, $(1 - B)^2$, $(1 - B)^3$, etc.

Let us now represent what will occur in a visual comparison between two straight lines which we shall call L_1 and L_2, where L_2 is invariable and L_1 has the following successive values: $L_1 = L_2$; $L_1 = 2L_2$; $L_1 = 3L_2$, etc. Let us start once again with these two lines divided into equal segments, each one of which can be a "point of encounter" in the sense indicated above. What is added in a comparison between L_1 and L_2 is that each encounter on L_1 can either correspond or not correspond to an encounter on L_2 and vice versa. We shall call these correspondences between points of encounter *couplings* and shall assume that the comparison will not give rise to relative overestimation or underestimation if the coupling is complete, whereas an incomplete coupling will involve a relative overestimation of the incompletely coupled line. In this case, there are encounters without coupling, i.e., overestimation by centration on one line which is not compensated by overestimation on the other line. The problem, then, is to calculate the probability of a complete coupling, and here again the solution is very simple.

Let us call p the probability that point A on one of the lines will be coupled with point B on the other line. If a second point of encounter C is introduced on this other line, the probability of a coupling between A and C will also be p, but the probability that A will simultaneously be coupled with B and with C will be p^2. The probability of a coupling between A on one line and B, C, and D on the other will be p^3, etc.

If $L_1 = L_2$ with n points on L_1 and m $(= n)$ points on L_2, the probability of a complete coupling will be:

$$(p^n)^m \text{ or } L_1 = L_2$$

If $L_1 = 2L_2$, the probability of a complete coupling will thus be:

$$[(p^n)p^n]^m = (p^m)^n = p^{m \cdot m}$$

Similarly, if $L_1 = 3L_2$, the probability of a complete coupling will be:

$$\{[(p^n)p^n]p^n\}^m = p^{m \cdot m}$$

In other words, the arithmetic progression of the lengths of L_1 (where $L_1 = L_2$, $2L_2$, $3L_2$, etc.) corresponds to the geometric progression of the probabilities of complete couplings and once again constitutes a logarithmic law.

It is immediately obvious that the logarithmic law which explains the relative overestimation of the greater of two compared lines involves a particular application of Weber's law, which is concerned with differential thresholds of perception and with just noticeable perceptual differences. Let us assume, for example, that the lines L_1 and L_2 differ by a constant X and that when these lines L_1 and L_2 are elongated progressively the absolute difference X remains invariant. As a function of the preceding schema, it is easy to see that this difference X will not remain perceptually identical. It will be distorted in proportion to the elongation of the lines L_1 and L_2. There is no point in providing the calculations here, since they have been published elsewhere [Piaget, 1955], but it is easy to see from the foregoing discussion of the probability of coupling, that Weber's law can be presented in logarithmic form.

Let us revert now to the law of relative centrations and see how it is explained by means of these probabilities of encounter and coupling, i.e., by the mechanisms of overestimation by centering, which appears to take into account all the "primary" illusions.

For clarity's sake, let us start by classifying the four possible varieties of couplings. If one compares two unequal lines $L_1 > L_2$, the following varieties of couplings can be distinguished:

1) The "couplings of difference" D between line L_2 and that part of line L_1 which surpasses L_2, i.e. $(L_1 - L_2)$. The couplings of difference will equal $(L_1 - L_2)L_2$, and it is immediately obvious that this product is the essential expression involved in the law of relative centrations.

2) The "couplings of resemblance" R between line L_2 and that part of line L_1 which is equal to L_2. These couplings will equal L_2^2.

3) The couplings D′ between that part of L_1 which is equal to L_2 and the virtual prolongation of L_2 up to equality with L_1, i.e. $(L_1 - L_2)$. These D′ couplings will thus be of the same value as D, i.e. $(L_1 - L_2)L_2$.

4) Finally, one can conceive of couplings D″ between part $(L_1 - L_2)$ of line L_1 and the virtual prolongation of L_2 cited above. The value of D″ will thus be $(L_1 - L_2)^2$.

In order to demonstrate the reasoning behind the law of relative centration, it can be formulated as follows:

$$P = \pm \frac{(L_1 - L_2)L_2}{S} \times \frac{nL}{L_{max}}.$$

It can be seen that the numerator of the first fraction, $(L_1 - L_2)L_2$, corresponds to the coupling of difference D which has just been described.

The surface S always corresponds to the entirety of possible couplings compatible with the junctions of the figure. In a closed figure such as a rectangle, the possible couplings are merely the couplings of difference D and of resemblance R. The surface of the rectangle $L_1 \times L_2$ can be formulated as $L_1L_2 = L_2{}^2 + (L_1 - L_2)L_2$, where $L_2{}^2 = R$ couplings and $(L_1 - L_2)L_2 = D$ couplings.

In open figures such as line $L_1 + L_2$, the surface $(L_1 + L_2)^2$ corresponds to all the couplings $D + R + D' + D''$ not only between L_1 and L_2 but also between L_1 and Lmax. In other words, the first fraction of the law $[(L_1 - L_2)L_2]/S$, merely expresses a probabilistic relationship: the relationship between the couplings of difference D, on which errors of overestimation are made, and the set of possible couplings.

The second fraction nL/Lmax expresses the relationship between the potential number of meeting points or couplings on the measured line L and on the total length Lmax. This relationship simply plays the role of a direction factor with respect to the first fraction [Piaget and Lambercier, 1944].

The significance of the law of relative centration thus becomes apparent. It expresses the proportion of possible couplings of difference D with respect to the figure as a whole. As it is these couplings that give rise to errors, it follows that this law is valid for all plane figures (which give rise to "primary" illusions) and it indicates the general shape of the error curve (the maxima and median null illusion) independently of the absolute value of these errors. The absolute value itself depends on the relative completeness of the couplings, so it is understandable that these "primary" errors diminish with age. This follows because, with increasing age, there is increasing visual exploratory activity and a consequent rise in the number of couplings.

As we have seen, however, there is a second category of

perceptual illusions: those which augment with age, either without interruption or with a plateau at around the age of eleven with a subsequent slight diminution. These errors cannot be accounted for by the law of relative centration, even though they are affected by it. They can be explained in the following manner. With age there is an increase in the perceptual activities of exploration and of comparison at increasing distances in space (spatial transports by means of visual displacements) and in time (temporal transports from prior to subsequent percepts and sometimes sets or "Einstellungen"). In general, these activities contribute to the diminution of perceptual errors, thanks to the increase of couplings. In some instances, however, they can give rise to contrasts or assimilations among distant elements which are not taken into account by young children and consequently do not give rise to errors. In these instances, we speak of "secondary" errors, since they constitute the indirect product of activities which normally lead to a diminution of errors.

A good example is provided by illusions of weight and their visual equivalent investigated by the Russian psychologist Usnadze [1939], which we have studied genetically in collaboration with Lambercier. Subjects are presented tachistoscopically with two circles, one 20 mm. in diameter and the other 28 mm. Subsequently, these circles are replaced with two circles of 24 mm. The circle which replaces the 20-mm. circle is overestimated by contrast with the original, and the circle which replaces the 28-mm. circle is underestimated. This illusion increases with age, even though in and of themselves the effects of contrast, which depend on the mechanism of relative centration, diminish with age. The reason for this paradox is simple. In order for a contrast to occur, the previously perceived elements (28 + 20 mm.) must be linked to the subsequent elements (24 + 24 mm.). This relationship occurs thanks to an activity which we have called "temporal transport," which increases with age, as has been demonstrated in many other experiments. Small children of five to eight years make fewer temporal transports, so that there is less contrast because fewer relationships are established, and even though the contrast may be greater in the child than in the adult when comparisons are made, the illusion will be weaker. But is it not arbitrary to assume that temporal transport is an "activity" that increases with age? No, and the best proof is that in the adult the illusion is not only stronger but it also disappears more quickly when the second presentation (24 + 24) is repeated several times. By contrast, in the child the illusion is weaker but lasts longer (slow extinction owing to perseveration). Temporal transport is thus an activity which can be blocked, and that is the best criterion of an activity.

Another striking example of an illusion that increases with age is the overestimation of vertical lines with respect to horizontals. In collaboration with A. Morf, we studied the figure "L" in its four possible positions: L ˥ ˩ Г. We found: (1) that the error with respect to the vertical increases with age; (2) that the error increases with exercise (five repetitions) instead of diminishing immediately, as is the case in primary illusions; (3) that the error depends on the order of presentation of the figures, as though there were a transfer of the mode of spatial transport (from below to above or from above to below).

Similarly, Wursten [1947], at our instigation, compared vertical and oblique lines of 5 cm. each, separated by an interval of 5 cm. and inclined at varying degrees. He found that small children of five to seven years were much more successful in their evaluations than adults. The error increases with age up to around nine to ten years and subsequently diminishes somewhat.

The increase of these errors with respect to vertical and oblique lines with increasing age can, it seems, be explained as follows. The perceptual space of the small child is less structured along horizontal and vertical coordinates than that of the adult, because such structuring presupposes the establishment of relationships between the object perceived and points of reference situated at distances beyond the boundaries of the figures. With increasing age, there is a constantly broader and more far-reaching frame of reference as a function of the establishment of perceptual relations. This leads to an ever-increasing qualitative contrast between horizontals and verticals. The error with respect to the vertical line is no doubt due to a difference in the distribution of the points of centration and of "encounters" on the vertical and on the horizontal lines. The upper and lower parts of the vertical line are not symmetrical from the perceptual point of view (the top is "open" while the bottom is "closed" toward the base), whereas the two halves of the horizontal line are perceptually symmetrical. The small child's space is less structured along coordinates, because his perceptual activity is not concerned with distant relationships. He is thus less sensitive to the qualitative difference between horizontal and vertical lines and to the perceptual asymmetry of the latter, since this asymmetry is a function of the general background of the figure.

In sum, in addition to the "primary" effects which stem from the law of relative centrations, there is a whole body of perceptual activities—transports, comparisons at a distance, transpositions, anticipations, etc.—which, in general, lead to the attenuation of primary errors but can provoke secondary errors when they relate elements at a distance giving rise to contrasts, etc. In other words, they give rise to illusions which would not be produced without the establishment of distant relationships.

It must, however, be understood that these perceptual activities in a sense stem from the primary effects, since the "encounters" and "couplings" associated with them are due to centrations and decentrations which constitute activities in themselves. At all levels perception is active and cannot be reduced to passive reception. As Karl Marx said in his objections to Feuerbach, sensibility must be considered as "the practical activity of man's senses."

NOTES

[1] Originally published in *Voprossi Psychkhologuii*, 1956.

[2] The operational construction of number is accomplished at the same age. Up until about the age of six or seven (at least for the children of Geneva), "figural" numbers already exist for small collections but without the character of conservation proper to operations. For example, place a row of six blue chips in front of the subject and ask him to match them with a row of six red chips. At first, he limits himself to constructing a row of the same length before achieving item-for-item correspondence of the chips. If the spaces between the chips in one row are then narrowed or widened, the subject of five to six years no longer believes that the two rows contain an equal number of chips. At about the age of seven, on the other hand, the succession of numbers is established, thanks to the operations which consist simultaneously of inclusive addition (class) and ordination (seriation) plus the inverse operations. These provide the conservation of the whole and means to distinguish a unit from the following term. The whole number can thus be conceived as a synthesis of the class and the asymmetrical relationship (order). Hence its simultaneous ordinal and cardinal character.

Most of our findings on this subject were originally published with A. Szeminska in 1940. [For some inexplicable reason Szeminska's name is not on the English (1952[a]) edition. Ed.]. These findings have since been substantiated by a Soviet child psychologist of renown, M. Kostiouk of Kiev.

CHAPTER 6

Genesis and Structure in the Psychology of Intelligence [1]

LET US START by defining the terms we shall use. We shall define structure in the broadest possible sense as a system which presents the laws or properties of a totality seen as a system. These laws of totality are different from the laws or properties of the elements which comprise the system. I must emphasize the fact that these systems are merely partial systems with respect to the whole organism or the mind. The concept of structure does not imply just any kind of totality and does not mean that everything is attached to everything else, as in Bichat's [1815] theory of the organism. We are concerned with a partial system, which, as a system, presents laws of totality distinct from the properties of its elements. The term "structure" remains vague, however, so long as the laws of totality are not specified. This is relatively easy to do in certain fields. For example, in mathematics the Bourbaki [2] structures can be reduced to algebraic structures, to structures of order, and to topological structures. The structures of group, field, or ring, concepts that have definite laws of totality are algebraic structures. The lattices, semilattices, etc., are structures of order. If we apply a broad definition to the concept of structure, the structures will have properties or laws that remain somewhat global, and in consequence their reduction to mathematical or physical constructs remains in the realm of wishful thinking. I am thinking of the concept of Gestalt which we need in psychology. I shall define it as an irreversible system whose composition is nonadditive by contrast with the above-mentioned logico-mathematical structures, which are rigorously reversible. However vague it may be, the concept of Gestalt does hold the promise of eventual conceptualization in mathematical or physical terms.

In defining "genesis," I should like to avoid being accused of constructing a vicious circle so I shall not say that it is simply the process of transition from one structure to another. Rather, genesis is a certain kind of transformation which stems from a state A and results in a state B, where state B is more stable than state A. When we speak of genesis in the field of psychology—and no doubt this is true of other fields also—we must first avoid any definition based on absolute beginnings. In psychology there are no absolute beginnings and genesis is always conceived as stemming from an initial state which may also comprise a structure. Consequently, genesis is simply a form of development. It does not, however, involve just any kind of development or a simple transformation. We can define genesis as a relatively determined system of transformations comprising a history and leading in a continuous manner from state A to state B, state B being more stable than the initial state and constituting an extension of it. For example, in biology, ontogenesis leads to the relatively stable state of adulthood.

1. HISTORICAL BACKGROUND

Now that these two terms have been defined, I should like to say a few quick words concerning the historical background of psychology, because this study, which is intended essentially as a point of departure for discussion, cannot possibly exhaust all the problems presented by the psychology of intelligence. These few words are necessary, however, because it must be emphasized that, unlike what Lucien Goldmann [1952] has shown in sociology, psychology did not stem from systems such as those of Hegel and Marx. It did not stem from systems that from the outset presented a relationship between the structural and the genetic aspects of phenomena. In psychology and biology, where the use of dialectic appeared relatively late, the first genetic theories, hence the first theories concerned with development, could be qualified as *genesis without structures*. This is the case, for example, in Lamarckian biology. For Lamarck, there are no limits to the organism's plasticity; it is constantly modified by environmental influences. There are thus no invariable internal structures, not even internal structures capable of resisting or entering into effective interaction with environmental influences.

In psychology there was, to begin with—if not a Lamarckian influence—at any rate, a state of mind altogether analogous to that of evolutionism in its earliest form. I am thinking, for example, of the associationism of Spencer, Taine, Ribot, etc., where the concept of evolution was applied to mental life: i.e., the conception of a plastic organism constantly modified through learning, through external influences, through exercise or "experience" in the empirical sense of the term. Certain current American learning theories were inspired by this concept. According to such theories, the organism is constantly modified by environmental influences with the sole exception of certain very limited innate structures which are actually confined to the instinctual needs. All the rest is pure plasticity without true structuralism.

After this first phase, there was an about-face in the direction this time of a *structuralism without genesis*. In biology the movement started with Weismann [1902] and has continued with his followers. In a certain limited sense, Weismann reverts to a kind of preformism. Evolution is merely apparent or results from the mixing of genes. Everything, however, is determined internally by certain structures which cannot be modified by environmental influences. In philosophy, the phenomenology of Husserl [1913], presented as an antipsychology, leads to an intuition of structures or of essences independent of all genesis. I mention Husserl here because he exerted an influence on the history of psychology. He is in part responsible for inspiring the Gestalt theory. This theory is the prototype of a structuralism without genesis, the structures being permanent and independent of development. I know very well that Gestalt theory has furnished concepts and interpretations of development itself, such as Koffka's [1928] excellent book on mental growth. Nevertheless, for him development is determined entirely by maturation, i.e., by a preformation which itself obeys Gestalt laws. Genesis remains secondary to the fundamental preformist perspective.

Having mentioned these two points of view—genesis without structure and structure without genesis—I will undoubtedly be expected to present you with the necessary synthesis: genesis and structure. However, I did not arrive at this conclusion through a taste for symmetry, as one does in a soundly traditional dissertation in philosophy. It has been imposed on me by the totality of facts which I have gathered in over forty years of research in child psychology. I must emphasize that this long inquiry has been undertaken without any prior hypothesis with respect to the relationship between genesis and structure. For a long time I did not even think explicitly about such problems. I envisaged the question only rather belatedly in 1949 as a result of a meeting of the Société Française de Philosophie, where I had the opportunity to discuss the results of the calculus of symbolic logic on the group of four transformations applied to the propositional operations which we shall discuss. After this exposition, Émile Bréhier intervened with his characteristic profundity to say that he would willingly accept a genetic psychology in this form, because the geneses of which I had spoken were always based on structures, and that genesis in consequence was subordinate to structure. I replied that I certainly agreed, provided there was true reciprocity (since every structure itself has a genesis) along the lines of a dialectical relationship without absolute primacy of one of the terms with respect to the other.

2. GENESIS EMANATES FROM A STRUCTURE AND CULMINATES IN A STRUCTURE

I shall now come to my theses. First thesis: *Genesis emanates from a structure and culminates in another structure*. The states A and B, mentioned before in my definition of genesis, are always structures. Let us take as an example the group of four transformations. This furnishes a highly significant model of structure in the field of intelligence. Its formation can be followed in children between twelve and fifteen years. Before the age of twelve, the child is unaware of any propositional logic. He is aware only of certain elementary forms of the logic of classes, with "inversion" as reversibility, and the logic of relations, with "reciprocity" as reversibility. As of the age of twelve, a new structure develops which reaches a stable equilibrium in adolescence at around fourteen to fifteen years. This new structure unifies the inversions and reciprocities in one system and its influence is very striking in all fields of formal intelligence at this level of development. This innovation is the group structure which presents four types of transformations: identical I, inverse N, reciprocal R, and correlative C. Let us take as a commonplace example the implication p implies q, whose inverse is p and not q and whose reciprocal is q implies p. We know that the operation p *not* q, reciprocated, will produce *not* p *and* q, which constitutes the inverse of q implies p, whose correlative is p implies q, the correlative being defined by the permutation of the *not* and the *and* (the dysjunctions and conjunctions). Thus we are dealing with a group of transformations, since each two-by-two composition of the transformations N, R, or C yields the third and the three together produce the identical transformation I, so that: $NR = C$; $NC = R$; $CR = N$; and $NRC = I$.

This structure is of great interest in the psychology of intelligence. It explains a phenomenon which otherwise would remain inexplicable. This is the appearance, at the age twelve to fifteen, of a series of new operational schemata whose origins are not immediately comprehensible and which are contemporaneous without at first sight appearing to be interrelated. For example, there is the concept of mathematical proportion which is taught only at around the age of eleven to twelve (if it could be comprehended earlier, it would certainly be introduced into the curriculum sooner). Secondly, there is the capacity to reason with two systems of reference at a time—for example, to solve a problem involving a snail advancing along a plank at the same time as the plank is being displaced in another direction or to comprehend systems of physical equilibrium (action and reaction, etc.). This structure, which I am taking as an example, does not appear out of the blue; it has a genesis, which is very interesting to trace. In this structure, there are two distinct and remarkable forms of reversibility: on the one hand, inversion, hence negation, and on the other hand, reciprocity, which is quite another thing. In a double system of reference, for example, the inverse operation will mark the return to the departure point on the plank, whereas reciprocity will be expressed by a compensation resulting from the movement of the plank with respect to reference points external to it. At this stage, reversibility by inversion and reversibility by reciprocity are united in a single total system, whereas for the child under twelve years these two forms of reversibility exist but they exist apart. A child of seven years is already capable of logical operations, but of operations which I shall call concrete, since they bear on objects and not on propositions. These concrete operations are operations of classes and relations, but they are not exhaustive. In analyzing them, you will discover that the operations of classes presuppose reversibility by inversion $(+a - a = 0)$ and that the operations of relations presuppose reversibility by reciprocity. These are two parallel systems which heretofore have not been interrelated, whereas with the appearance of the INRC group they become fused into a whole.

Thus the structure of the INRC group, which appears at around twelve years, is anticipated by more elementary structures which do not have the same character as the total structure but have partial characteristics which will become synthesized subsequently into a final structure. Analysis of the groupings of classes and relations employed by the seven-to-twelve-year-old shows that they themselves are prepared for by even more elementary structures (which are not yet logical but prelogical) in the form of articulated intuitions and representative regulations, which are only semireversible. The genesis of these structures reverts back to the sensorimotor level, which precedes language, where there is already a whole structuring in the form of the construction of space, groups of displacement, permanent objects, etc., a structuring which can be considered the departure point for all subsequent logic. In other words, whenever one is dealing with a structure in the psychology of intelligence, its genesis can be traced to other more elementary structures which do not constitute absolute beginnings themselves but have a prior genesis in even more elementary structures, and so on ad infinitum.

I say ad infinitum, but the psychologist will stop at birth. He will stop at the sensorimotor level, and at this level there is, of course, the whole biological problem because the neural structures themselves have their genesis, and so it continues.

3. EVERY STRUCTURE HAS A GENESIS

Second thesis: So far I have said that every genesis emanates from a structure and culminates in another structure. Conversely, *every structure has a genesis*. You will see right away from what I have said so far that this reciprocity is inevitable once such structures are analyzed. The clearest result of our research on the psychology of intelligence is that even the structures most necessary to the adult mind, such as the logico-mathematical structures, are not innate in the child; they are built up little by little. Such fundamental structures as, for example, those of transitivity or inclusion (which implies that a total class contains more elements than the subclass which it comprises), of the commutativity of elementary additions, etc., which for us are absolutely obvious and necessary, are built up only little by little in the child. This is true even of the biunivocal and reciprocal correspondences, of the conservation of wholes when the spatial disposition of the elements is transformed, etc. There are no innate structures: every structure presupposes a construction. All these constructions originate from prior structures and revert, in the final analysis, as I said before, to the biological problem.

In short, genesis and structure are indissociable. They are temporally indissociable, for between the point of departure of one structure and the point of arrival of another more complex structure there must of necessity be a process of construction, which is genesis. There is thus never the one without the other, but they cannot be conceptualized together at the same moment because genesis is the passage from a prior to a subsequent state. How, then, can we conceive of this relationship between structure and genesis in a more intimate fashion? Here again, I shall take up the hypothesis of equilibrium which I imprudently tossed into the discussion yesterday and which gave rise to diverse reactions. I hope to be able to justify it a little better today in this exposition.

4. EQUILIBRIUM

First of all, what do we mean by equilibrium in psychology? In psychology we must beware of words borrowed from other much more precise disciplines, since they may give the illusion of precision if the concepts are not carefully defined. Otherwise, we may say too much or say things that are not verifiable.

In order to define equilibrium, I shall make use of three characteristics. First, equilibrium is notable for its stability. But let us note at the outset that stability does not signify immobility. As you know very well, there are in chemistry and in physics mobile equilibria characterized by transformations in opposite directions that are compensated in a stable fashion. The concept of mobility thus does not contradict the concept of stability; equilibrium can be both mobile and stable. In the field of intelligence we have great need of this concept of mobile equilibrium. An operational system, for example, is a system of actions, a series of essentially mobile operations which nevertheless can remain stable in the sense that, once constituted, the structure which determines them will not become modified.

Secondly, every system is subject to external intrusion which tends to modify it. We shall say that there is equilibrium when this external intrusion is compensated by the actions of the subject. The idea of compensation seems to me fundamental in the definition of psychological equilibrium.

Finally, the third point I should like to emphasize is that equilibrium, thus defined, is not something passive but, on the contrary, something essentially active; the greater the equilibrium, the more activity is required. It is very difficult to conserve equilibrium from the mental point of view. The moral equilibrium of a personality presupposes force of character in order to resist temptation, to conserve the values one holds, etc. Equilibrium is synonymous with activity. In the field of intelligence the same holds true. A structure is in equilibrium to the extent that an individual is sufficiently active to be able to counter all intrusion with external compensations. Moreover, the intrusion will ultimately be anticipated by thought. Potential intrusion can, at the same time, be anticipated and compensated, thanks to the inverse or reciprocal operations.

Thus defined, the concept of equilibrium seems to have particular value with respect to the synthesis of genesis and structure, inasmuch as the concept of equilibrium encompasses the concepts of compensation and of activity. If we consider a structure of intelligence, a logico-mathematical structure of whatever kind (a structure of pure logic, of class, classification, relation, etc., or a propositional operation), we first, of course, find activity, since we are dealing with operations, but above all we find the fundamental characteristic of logico-mathematical structures, namely, reversibility. A logical transformation can, in effect, always be inversed by a transformation in the opposite direction or reciprocated by a reciprocal transformation. Now it is obvious that this reversibility is very close to what earlier I called compensation in the field of equilibrium. Nonetheless, there are two distinct realities involved. When we are dealing with a psychological analysis we are always obliged to reconcile two systems: that of awareness and that of behavior or psychophysiology. On the plane of awareness we have to do with implications, while on the behavioral or psychophysiological plane we have to do with causal series.[8] I can say that the reversibility of operations, i.e., of logico-mathematical structures, is the property of the structures on the plane of implication, but in order to understand how genesis leads to these structures we must have recourse to causal language. It is here that the concept of equilibrium as I have defined it enters in as a system of progressive compensations. When the compensations are achieved, i.e., when equilibrium is attained, the structure is constituted in its reversible state.

5. EXAMPLE OF LOGICO-MATHEMATICAL STRUCTURES

In order to clarify matters, let us take an altogether banal example of logico-mathematical structures. I shall take it from one of our current experiments in child psychology: the conservation of matter in a ball of clay subjected to a certain number of transformations. The child is presented with two balls of clay of the same size; then one of the two balls is elongated in the form of a sausage. The child is then asked if the two clay objects still represent the same quantity of clay. We know from numerous experiments that, to begin with, the child denies the conservation of matter. He imagines either that there is more clay in the sausage because it is longer or that there is less because it is thinner. Not until the age of seven or eight years will he concede that the quantity of matter has not changed; not until a little later will he recognize the conservation of weight, and not until around the age of eleven or twelve will he recognize the conservation of volume.

Now the conservation of matter is a structure—or at least the index of a structure, which, of course, rests on a whole operational group of greater complexity—whose reversibility is manifested by the compensations exercised by the operations. Where does this structure come from? Current developmental or genetic theories of the psychology of intelligence either consecutively or simultaneously employ three factors. The first is maturation—an internal, structural, hereditary factor. The second is the influence of the physical environment, of experience or exercise. The third is social transmission. Let us see how these factors fare in the case of our ball of modeling clay. First of all, maturation. Certainly, it plays its role, but it is far from enough to solve our problem. The proof is that conservation is not manifested at the same age in different environments. One of my students from Iran devoted her thesis to various experiments in Teheran and in the remote countryside of her country. In Teheran she found compensation occurred at the same age levels as in Geneva and Paris; in the remote countryside she noted a considerable delay. Consequently, maturation alone is not responsible. The social environment, exercise, and experience must be taken into account. The second factor, physical experience, certainly plays its part. I have no doubt that as a function of manipulating objects one arrives at concepts of conservation. But in the specific case of the conservation of matter, I see two problems. First of all, this matter which supposedly is conserved by the child before weight or volume is a reality which can be neither perceived nor measured. What is a quantity of matter whose weight and volume vary? It is not something accessible to the senses: it is pure substance. It is very interesting to see how the child starts with the notion of substance, like the pre-Socratics, before arriving at conservations verifiable by measurements. Actually, this conservation of substance is empty of form. It is not supported by anything from the point of view of possible measurement or perception. I do not see how experience could impose the idea of the conservation of substance before the conservation of weight or of volume. It is enforced by logical structuring much more than by experience; in any event, it is not due to experience alone.

In addition, we have conducted learning experiments by the method of teaching the results. These experiments have accelerated the process but are unable to introduce a new logical structure from without.

The third factor, social transmission, certainly also plays a basic role, but while it constitutes a necessary condition, it is not a sufficient condition. First of all, conservation is not taught; in general, teachers do not even suspect that it might be taught to young children. Secondly, when knowledge is transmitted to a child, experience shows that either it falls on deaf ears or, if it is understood, it is restructured. This restructuring requires internal logic.

I shall say, then, that each of these factors plays a part but that no one of them is sufficient.

6. CASE STUDY

Now I shall draw on the concept of equilibrium or equilibration. In order to give more concrete content to what up till now has been merely abstract, I should like to envisage a more precise model, which, in a particular case, can be only a probabilistic model. It will show you how the subject passes progressively from an unstable to a more and more stable state of equilibrium, up to the stage of complete compensation which characterizes true equilibrium. Because it can be suggestive, I shall borrow the language of game theory. In the development of intellectual structures, four phases can be distinguished, each of which can be called a "strategy." The first phase has the highest probability at the outset; the second phase becomes the most probable as a function of the results of the first but does not have the highest probability to start with; the third becomes the most probable as a function of the second, and so it continues. There is thus sequential probability. In studying the reactions of children of different ages, one observes that in the first phase the child uses only a single dimension. He will say: "There is more clay here than there because it's bigger, it's longer." If you elongate the sausage further, he will say: "There's even more because it's even longer." As it becomes elongated, the piece of clay naturally becomes thinner, but the child considers only the one dimension and totally neglects the other. It is true that certain children refer to the breadth, but this is rare. These children will say: "There is less clay because it's thinner; there is even less because it's even thinner," but they will forget the length. In both cases, the child is unaware of conservation and refers to only one dimension, either one or the other, not both at the same time. I think this first phase has the highest probability at the outset. Why? To take a quantified example, let us say arbitrarily that the length yields a probability of .7, assuming that in seven out of ten cases length is mentioned, while breadth is mentioned in three cases, and hence has a probability of .3. From the moment the child reasons about one dimension and not about the other and judges them to be independent, the probability of both at the same time will be .21 and in all intermediate cases it will be between .21 and .3 or .21 and .7. Two at a time is more difficult than one alone. The most probable reaction at the point of departure is thus centration on a single dimension.

Now let us examine the second phase. The child will reverse his judgment. Take the child who reasons about length. He tells you: "It's still more but it's longer." However, it becomes probable—not at the outset but as a function of the first phase —that at a given moment he will adopt an inverse attitude. This is so for two reasons. First of all, there is the factor of perceptual contrast. If you continue to elongate the clay up to the point where it turns into spaghetti, he will end up by telling you: "Oh no, now there's less because it's too thin." Thus he

becomes aware of the thinness which heretofore he had neg-
lected. He had, of course, perceived it, but had conceptually
ignored it. The second factor is subjective dissatisfaction. As a
function of constantly repeating, "There is more because it's
longer," the child begins to doubt himself. He is like the sage
who starts doubting his own theory when it is too readily
applicable in all instances. The child will have more doubts at
the tenth affirmation than at the first or second. For these two
reasons it is highly probable that at a given moment he will give
up envisaging the length and will start to reason about the
breadth. But at this stage of the process he reasons about the
breadth just as he reasoned about the length. He forgets the
length and continues to consider merely a single dimension.
This second phase is, of course, shorter than the first and in a
few cases consists of only a few minutes.

In the third phase the child will reason about the two dimensions at once. First of all, though, he will oscillate between the
two. Since up to now he has sometimes invoked length, sometimes breadth, every time you present him with a new device or
transform the shape of the clay, he will choose either the length
or the breadth. He will say: "I don't know. It's more because
it's longer . . . no, it's thinner so it's less . . ." This will lead
him—and we are dealing here not with an *a priori* but with a
sequential probability as a function of this particular situation
—to discovering the interdependence of the two transformations. He discovers that to the extent that the ball becomes
elongated, it becomes thinner, and that each transformation of
length involves a transformation of breadth and vice versa.

From then on, the child starts to reason about the transformations, whereas up till then he reasoned only about each
independent configuration, first of the ball, then of the sausage.
As soon as he starts to reason about length and breadth at the
same time, hence about the interdependence of the two varia-
bles, he will start to reason in terms of transformations. In
consequence, he will discover that the two variations are inverse
to each other, i.e., that as the clay lengthens it becomes propor-

tionately thinner, and as it broadens it becomes proportionately shorter. In other words, he is on his way toward compensation. When he has started in this direction, the structure will become crystallized. Since the same clay has just been transformed without anything being added or subtracted, it has been transformed in two dimensions which are inverse to each other so that whatever the ball gains in length it loses in breadth and vice versa.

The child now finds a reversible system, and we have reached the fourth phase. This is an example of a progressive equilibration and—I must emphasize—of an equilibration which is not preformed. The second or third stage increases in probability as a function of the immediately preceding stage, not as a function of the point of departure. Equilibration is thus a process with sequential probability which finally results in a necessity at the point where the child comprehends compensation and where equilibrium is manifested directly by the system of implication which I previously called reversibility. At this level of equilibrium he attains stability, since he no longer has any reason to deny the conservation, but sooner or later the structure will, of course, be integrated into subsequent, more complex systems.

It is in this manner, it seems to me, that an extratemporal structure can develop from a temporal process. In temporal genesis, the stages merely obey increasing probabilities, all of which are determined by a temporal order of succession, but once the equilibrated structure is crystallized, it forces itself as necessary on the subject's mind. This necessity is the sign of the completion of the structure, which then becomes extratemporal. I am intentionally using terms which may appear contradictory. If you prefer, I shall say that we arrive *a priori* at a kind of necessity, but it is an *a priori* which is constituted only at the end not at the point of departure, as a resultant and not as a source, and hence retains only the concept of necessity and not that of preformation.

NOTES

[1] Lecture given at Cerisy under the auspices of the École Pratique des Hautes Études and published as, "Entretiens sur les notions de 'genèse' et de 'structure'." in *Congrès et Colloques*, Paris: Mouton et Cie, 1964, Vol. VIII.

[2] A school of predominantly French mathematicians all of whom publish under the fictitious name of Bourbaki. Ed.

[3] Perhaps what Piaget means here is that it makes little sense to talk about thoughts *causing* one another, since the connotation is that of physical or material things acting upon one another. To say that thoughts imply one another removes this ambiguity, since implication has logical and not physicalistic connotations. Ed.

Bibliographical
References

ABELE, J., and MALVAUX, P. *Vitesse et univers relativiste.* Paris: Sedes, 1954.

APOSTEL, L. "Logique, langage et théorie de l'information." In J. Piaget (ed)., *Études d'épistémologie génétique*, Vol. 3. Paris: P.U.F.,* 1957.

ASHBY, W. R. *Dynamics of the Cerebral Cortex: Automatic Development of Equilibrium in Self-organizing Systems.* Psychometrica, 1947, 12, 135–40.

BALDWIN, J. M. *Mental Development in the Child and the Race.* New York: Macmillan, 1906.

———. *Thought and Things or Genetic Logic.* New York: Macmillan, Vol. 1, 1906; Vol. 2, 1908.

BAYES, T. "An Essay Towards Solving a Problem in the Doctrine of Chances." *Phil. Trans. Rog. Soc.*, 1763, I. iii, p. 370.

BERLYNE, D., and PIAGET, J. "Théorie du comportement et opérations." In J. Piaget (ed.), *Études d'épistémologie génétique*, Vol. 12. Paris: P.U.F., 1960.

BERTALANFFY, L. V. *Problems of Life.* London: C. A. Watts, 1952.

———. "Comments on Professor Piaget's Paper." In J. M. Tanner and B. Inhelder (eds.), *Discussions on Child Development*, Vol. 4. London: Tavistock, 1960.

BICHAT, X. *Physiological Researches on Life and Death.* London: Longman, Hurst, Rees, Orme, and Browne, 1815.

BOOLE, G. *The Laws of Thought.* New York: Dover, 1951 (American printing of the 1854 edition).

BORING, E. G. *A History of Experimental Psychology.* (2nd ed.) New York: Appleton, 1950.

BOVET, P. *The Child's Religion.* New York: Dutton, 1928.

BROUWER, L. E. J. "Consciousness, Philosophy, and Mathematics." *Proceedings of the 10th International Congress of Philosophy.* Amsterdam: 1949, 1235–49.

* Presses Universitaires de France.

BRUNER, J. S., and POSTMAN, L. "Perception, Cognition and Behavior." *J. Pers.* 1949, 18, 206–23.

BÜHLER, CHARLOTTE. *Kindheit und Jugend. Genese des Bewusstseins.* (3rd ed.) Leipzig: Herzel, 1931.

BURT, C. *Mental Tests.* Edinburgh: Brown, 1913.

CLAPARÈDE, E. *Le Développement mental.* Neuchâtel: Delachaux et Niestlé, 1951.

DEUTSCHE, J. M. "The Development of Children's Concepts of Causal Relations." *Univ. Minn. Inst. Child Welf. Monogr.*, 1937, 39, 144–49.

ERIKSON, E. H. *Childhood and Society.* (2nd ed.) New York: Norton, 1963.

FESTINGER, L. *A Theory of Cognitive Distonance.* Evanston, Illinois: Rowe, Peterson, 1957.

FREUD, S. "The Interpretation of Dreams." *The Basic Writings of Sigmund Freud.* New York: Modern Library, 1938.

GESELL, A. L. *The Embryology of Behavior.* New York: Harper, 1945.

GOLDMANN, L. *Sciences humaines et philosophie.* Paris: P.U.F., 1952.

GONSETH, F. *Les Mathématiques et la réalité.* Paris: Alcan, 1936.

GRIZE, J. B. "Du Groupement au nombre." In J. Piaget (ed.), *Études d'épistémologie génétique*, Vol. XIII. Paris: P.U.F., 1961.

HALL, G. S. *Adolescence.* New York: Appleton, 1908. 2 vols.

HOPPE, F. "Erfolg und Misserfolg." *Psychol. Forsch.*, 1930, 14, 89–174.

HUSSERL, E. "Ideen zu einer reinen Phänomenologie und phänomenologische Philosophie." *Jahrbuch für Philosophie und phänomenologische Forschung.* I. Halle: Niemeyer, 1913.

INHELDER, BÄRBEL, and PIAGET, J. *The Growth of Logical Thinking from Childhood to Adolescence.* New York: Basic Books, 1958.

INHELDER, BÄRBEL. *Le Diagnostic du raisonnement chez les débiles mentaux.* (2nd ed.) Neuchâtel: Delachaux & Niestlé, 1963.

ISAACS, N. "Children's 'Why' Questions." Appendix to Susan Isaacs, *Intellectual Growth in Young Children.* New York: Harcourt, Brace, 1930.

JAMES, W. "Thought before Language: A Deaf-Mute's Recollections." *Philosophical Review*, 1892, 1, 613–24.

———. *The Principles of Psychology.* Vol. II. New York: Dover, 1950.

JANET, P. *L'Évolution de la mémoire et de la notion du temps.* Paris: Éditions Chahine, 1928.

———. *L'Évolution psychologique de la personalité.* Paris: Éditions Chahine, 1929.

KOFFKA, K. *The Growth of the Mind.* (2nd ed.) London: Routledge & Kegan Paul, 1928.

LAURENDEAU, MONIQUE, and PINARD, A. *La Pensée causale.* Paris: P.U.F., 1962.

LEWIN, K. *A Dynamic Theory of Personality.* New York and London: McGraw-Hill, 1935.

———. "Behavior and Development as a Function of the Total Situation." In L. Carmichael (ed.), *Manual of Child Psychology*. New York: Wiley, 1954.

McCulloch, W. S., and Pitts, W. "A Logical Calculus of the Ideas Imminent in Nervous Activity." *Bull. Math. Biophys.*, 1943, 5, 115–33.

Mead, G. H. *The Social Psychology of George Herbert Mead*. Chicago: University of Chicago Press, 1956.

Payot, J. *The Education of the Will*. New York: Funk & Wagnalls, 1909.

Piaget, J. "L'Adaptation de la limnaea stagnalis aux milieux lacustres de la Suisse romande." *Revue Suisse de Zoologie*, 1929, 36, 263–531. (a)

———. "Les races lacustres de la limnaea stagnalis, Recherches sur les rapports de l'adaptation héréditaire avec le milieu." *Bull. Biologique de France et de Belgique*, 1929, LXIII, 429–55. (b)

———. "Children's Philosophies." In C. Murchison (ed.), *Handbook of Child Psychology*. Worcester, Mass: Clark University Press, 1931.

———. *Le Développement de la notion de temps chez l'enfant*. Paris: P.U.F., 1946. (a)

———. *Les Notions de mouvement et de vitesse chez l'enfant*. Paris: P.U.F., 1946. (b)

———. *The Moral Judgment of the Child*. Glencoe, Illinois: Free Press, 1948.

———. *The Psychology of Intelligence*. London: Routledge & Kegan Paul, 1950.

———. *Judgment and Reasoning in the Child*. London: Routledge & Kegan Paul, 1951. (a)

———. *The Child's Conception of Physical Causality*. London: Routledge & Kegan Paul, 1951. (b)

———. *The Child's Conception of the World*. London: Routledge & Kegan Paul, 1951. (c)

———. *Play, Dreams and Imitation in Childhood*. New York: Norton, 1951. (d)

———. *The Child's Conception of Number*. New York: Humanities Press, 1952. (a)

———. *The Language and Thought of the Child*. London: Routledge & Kegan Paul, 1952. (b)

———. *The Origins of Intelligence in Children*. New York: International Universities Press, 1952. (c)

———. *The Construction of Reality in the Child*. New York: Basic Books, 1954.

———. "Essai d'une nouvelle interprétation probabiliste des effets de centration, de la loi de Weber et de celle des centrations relatives." *Arch. de Psychol.*, 1955, XXXV, 1–24.

———. "Logique et équilibre dans les comportements du sujet." In J. Piaget (ed.), *Études d'épistémologie génétique*, Vol. II. Paris: P.U.F., 1957.

———. *Les Mécanismes perceptifs*. Paris: P.U.F., 1961.

PIAGET, J., and DENIS-PRINZHORN, MARIANNE. "L'estimation perceptive des côtés du rectangle." *Arch. de Psychol.*, 1953, XXXIV, 109–31.

PIAGET, J., FELLER, YVONNE, and McNEAR, ELISABETH. "Essai sur la perception des vitesses chez l'enfant et chez l'adulte. *Arch. de Psychol.*, 1958, 36, 253–327.

PIAGET, J., and INHELDER, BÄRBEL. *Le Développement des quantités physiques chez l'enfant*. Paris: Delachaux et Niestlé, 1941.

———. *La Genèse de l'idée de hasard chez l'enfant*. Paris: P.U.F., 1951.

———. *The Child's Conception of Space*. London: Routledge & Kegan Paul, 1956.

———. *La Genèse des structures logiques élémentaires*. Neuchâtel: Delachaux & Niestlé, 1959.

———. "Les images mentales." In P. Fraisse and J. Piaget (eds.), *Traité de Psychologie*, Vol. VII. Paris: P.U.F., 1963.

PIAGET, J., and LAMBERCIER, M. "Essai sur un effet d''Einstellung' survenant au cours de perceptions visuelles successives (Effet Usnadze)." *Arch. de Psychol.*, 1944, XXX, 139–96.

PIAGET, J., and MORF, A. "Les préinférences perceptives et leurs relations avec les schèmes sensori-moteurs et opératoires." In J. Piaget (ed.), *Études d'épistémologie génétique*, Vol. VI. Paris: P.U.F., 1958.

PIAGET, J., BANG, V., and MATALON, B. "Note on the Law of the Temporal Maximum of Some Optico-geometric Illusions." *Amer. J. Psychol.*, 1958, 71, 277–82.

POINCARÉ, H. *Science and Method*. London: Nelson, 1908.

RAPAPORT, D. "The Autonomy of the Ego." *Bull. Menninger Clinic*, 1951, 15, 113–23.

REY, A. *L'Intelligence pratique chez l'enfant*. Paris: Alcan, 1935.

STERN, CLARA, and STERN, W. *Errinerung, Aussage, und Lüge in der frühen Kindheit*. (4th ed.) Leipzig: Barth, 1931.

TOURNAY, A. *Sémiologie du sommeil*. Paris: G. Doin & Cie, 1934.

USNADZE, D. "Untersuchungen zur Psychologie der Einstellung." *Acta Psychol.*, 1939, 4, 323–60.

WALLON, H. *Les origines de la pensée Chez l'enfant*. Paris: P.U.F., 1945.

WATSON, J. B. *Psychology from the Standpoint of a Behaviorist*. Philadelphia & London: Lippincott, 1919.

WATSON, J. B., and MORGAN, J. J. B. "Emotional Reactions and Psychological Experimentation." *Amer. J. Psychol.*, 1917, 28, 163–74.

WEISMANN, A. *Vorträge über Descendenztheorie—die Keimplasmatheorie*. Jena: Fischer, 1902.

WHITEHEAD, A. N., and RUSSELL, B. *Principia Mathematica*. Cambridge, England: University Press, Vol. 1, 1910; Vol. 2, 1912; Vol. 3, 1913.

WURSTEN, H. "L'évolution des comparaisons de l'enfant à l'adulte." *Arch. de Psychol.*, 1947, XXXII, 1–144. Paris: P.U.F.

Biographical Note

꧁ JEAN PIAGET was born in Neuchâtel in 1896. The son of a well-known historian, Piaget demonstrated a rare precocity by undertaking and publishing a number of zoological studies before the age of sixteen. At the age of twenty-one he attained the European equivalent of an M.A. in natural science and the following year received his doctorate with a thesis dealing with the distribution of mollusks in the Alps. Soon afterward he received a second doctorate in logic and philosophy.

Piaget's diverse interests led him to do postdoctoral work with the psychiatrist, Bleuler, in Zurich and with Dr. Simon in Paris. It was during an attempt to standardize Burt's reasoning tests upon Parisian children that the zoologist and philosopher was transformed into the child psychologist and epistemologist who was to gain world-wide recognition before the age of thirty. After his work in Paris, Piaget was successively Director of Research at the Rousseau Institute in Geneva, Privat Docent at the Faculty of Science of the University of Geneva, Professor of Psychology and of the Philosophy of Science at the University of Neuchâtel, Professor of General Psychology at the University of Lausanne, Professor of Sociology and of Experimental Psychology at the University of Geneva. He was named Titular Professor of Genetic Psychology at the Sorbonne in 1952. Piaget is currently codirector of the Institute of Educational Science in Geneva, as well as Professor of Experimental Psychology at the Faculty of Science at the University of Geneva.

Piaget is an innovator. He has devoted his exceptional research and theoretical talents to the systematic understanding of the mental evolution of the child, as well as to problems of epistemology. He has been extraordinarily prolific, and his current bibliography totals to more than eighteen thousand printed pages (the equivalent of seventy-five two-hundred-fifty-page books!). Many of his works have been translated into numerous languages and some of them are now regarded as classics in the field. Piaget has received honorary degrees from universities around the world, including, most recently, the University of Pennsylvania. He is the founder of the Center for the Study of Genetic Epistemology in Geneva, which each year brings together scholars from all over the world to deal with problems of epistemology. Under Piaget's editorship, the Center has published more than twenty volumes of original research on epistemological problems.

Index of Names

Abele, J. 86
Apostel, L. 108
Ashby, W. R. 108, 109

Baldwin, J. M. xiv, 20
Bang, V. 109
Bayes, T. 109
Berlyne, D. 81
Bertalanffy, L. V. 101, 103
Beth, E. W. 83
Bichat, X. 143
Bleuler, E. 163
Boole, G. xiv, 120
Boring, E. G. xvi
Bovet, P. 20, 36, 67
Bréhier, E. 146
Brouwer, L. E. J. 82
Bruner, J. S. 106
Bühler, C. 68
Burt, C. 93, 163

Claparède, E. 6, 34, 59, 100

Darwin, C. x
Denis-Prinzhorn, M. 132
Deutsche, J. M. 87

Einstein, A. xv, 84, 85
Elvin, H. L. 77
Erikson, E. H. xix

Feller, Y. 85
Festinger, L. xvii
Feuerbach, L. A. 141
Freud, S. ix, x, 100

Gesell, A. L. 119
Goldmann, L. 145

Gonseth, F. 127
Grize, J. B. 83

Hall, G. S. xi
Hegel, G. W. F. 145
Helmholtz, H. 106
Hoppe, F. 72 (notes only)
Husserl, E. 146

Inhelder, B. 44, 80, 93, 96, 123,
    124, 125, 127
Isaacs, N. S. 78

James, W. 26, 59
Janet, P. 20, 100

Kant, I. xv
Koffka, K. 146

Lamarck, J. 145
Lambercier, M. 108, 138, 139
Laurendeau, M. 87 (notes only)
Lewin, K. 72, 100

Malvaux, P. 86
Marx, K. xv, 128, 141, 145
Matalon, B. 109
McCulloch, W. S. 120
McNear, E. 85
Mead, G. H. 72 (notes only)
Morf, A. 106, 140
Morgan, J. J. B. 71 (notes only)

Payot, J. 59
Pinard, A. 87 (notes only)
Pitts, W. 120
Poincaré, H. 82

Postman, L. 106
Pythagoras 43

Quine, W. V. O. 83

Rapaport, D. 73 (notes only)
Rey, A. 30
Ribot, T. A. 145
Russell, B. 82

Simon, T. 73, 163
Spencer, H. 145
Stern, C. 37

Stern, W. 37
Szeminska, A. 142

Taine, H. A. 145
Tournay, A. 119

Usnadze, D. 139

Wallon, H. 119
Watson, J. B. 71, 89
Weber, E. H. 134, 136, 137
Weismann, A. 145
Whitehead, A. N. 82
Wursten, H. 140

Subject Index

Accommodation xvi, 8, 18, 30, 64, 103; reciprocal 12, 54, 103
Adaptation 8, 18, 68, 69, 91
Adolescence xii, xiv, xix, 5, 6, 15, 60, 61, 63–69, 72, 147
Affectivity xviii, 4, 15, 16, 33, 34, 38, 41, 54, 55, 60, 61, 64, 69, 70, 102
Animism 25–27, 42
Artificialism 27, 42
Assimilation xvi, 8–12, 18, 22–24, 27–30, 34, 42, 43, 54, 64, 103
Atomism 43–46

Causality, schema of 13–16, 28, 41, 42, 46, 104
Circular reactions 11, 71
Concept
    of class 48, 52; of number 49, 53, 72, 82, 83, 116; sensori-motor
    12; of seriation 48–51, 53, 54; of space 47, 84–86; of speed 47,
    84–86; of time 47, 84–86; of volume 51; of weight 51
Conservation 40, 43–46, 79, 80, 112, 121, 123, 125, 127, 130, 142, 150,
    152–157
Constraint, material 21; psychological 20–21
Cooperation 6, 20, 39, 41, 54, 57, 65, 66, 69, 98
Couplings 110, 111, 135–141

Egocentrism 13–16, 18, 21, 26–30, 40–42, 46, 52, 64–66
Encounters 110, 111, 135–137, 141
Equilibrium
    cognitive 104, 109, 111, 114; mobile 4, 33, 109, 151; percep-
    tive 110–113; permanent 54; stable 4, 7, 33, 114, 147, 151
Errors (perceptual)
    primary 138, 141; secondary 139
Experiments, mental 17

Finalism 26, 27, 29, 42
Force, idea of 28

Genesis x, xxi, xxii, 81, 86, 90, 143–152, 157

Identification 42, 43
Illusions, primary, secondary 138–141
Image, mental 90, 122

Imitation
    deferred 90, 122; development of 19, 117; sensori-motor 19
Indices 91, 99, 153
Intelligence
    logical 8; sensori-motor and practical 8, 11, 12, 22, 29–30, 89, 94
Interest 5, 7, 33–36, 38, 59, 71, 102
Intuition 24, 30–33, 48–49, 148

Justice, concepts of 57

Language
    consequences of 17; functions of 19–21; spontaneous 19–21
Lattices 82, 92, 95, 97, 121, 125, 143
Law of relative centrations 134, 137–139, 141
Life plan 65–69, 73
Limraea Stagnalis 118
Logic
    of action 58, 79; formal 88, 125; propositional xiii, 63, 88, 91,
       92, 94, 95, 114, 125, 126, 147; of values 58

Maturation xvi, xvii, xxi, xxiii, 60, 103, 119, 120, 146, 153
Morals 37, 54–58, 60
Motives 6, 15

Narcissism 16, 17
Needs 4, 6, 7, 9, 34, 35, 102, 130

Object
    choice 16, 17; schema of 14, 16, 113
Operations
    combinatory 96–98, 125, 126; concrete 48, 64, 78, 92, 105, 124,
       127; formal 64–65, 78, 106; genesis of 48, 49; groupings of
       54–55, 58, 82; multiplicative 92; reversible 50, 55, 78, 80–82,
       113, 114, 121–123, 130, 152

Perception xxi, 8, 9, 16, 31, 32, 62, 85, 90, 100, 105, 106, 108, 109,
    116–118, 131, 136, 141, 154
Personality xviii, xix, 6, 64–66, 69
Play
    exercise 23; symbolic 23, 29, 64, 89, 90, 122; with rules 23
Probability, sequential 155, 156, 159

Reasoning 4, 50, 60, 62, 63, 95, 96, 125, 126
Reflection 29, 39, 40, 41, 61, 63–65
Reflex apparatus 9
Regulations 35, 36, 58, 59, 100, 102, 105, 114, 149
Respect
    mutual 38, 55–57; unilateral 37, 38, 54–57
Reversibility
    by negation 124, 130, 148; by reciprocity 121, 124, 130, 147, 148

Schemata
    of action 11, 12, 26, 32, 46, 48, 64, 106; sensori-motor 10, 30, 32,
       46, 89

Self xviii, xix, 12, 13, 16, 21–23, 27, 29, 35, 54, 55, 64–66, 69, 72, 79
Signals 91, 99
Signs, collective 91
Space
    practical schema of 14, 47
Stages, developmental 5, 6, 58, 107
States 179–81
Strategies 109, 111, 112
Structures
    construction of 77, 78, 81, 82, 150; genesis of 81, 100, 144, 147–
        149, 152; logico-mathematical 77, 81, 83, 105–106, 113, 114; pre-
        logical 78, 104–107, 148; variable 5
Symbols 23, 89
Symbolic function 91

Thought
    egocentric 23, 25, 64, 79; formal 62–69, 126; verbal 24, 29, 78

Values, personal 55, 58, 65

Will 34, 37, 41, 54, 55, 58–60, 65, 102

JEAN PIAGET was born in Neuchâtel in 1896. Before the age of sixteen he published a number of zoölogical studies and several years later received doctorates in natural science and philosophy. Piaget gained world-wide recognition before the age of thirty as a child psychologist and epistemologist. He is currently co-director of the Institute of Educational Science in Geneva, as well as Professor of Experimental Psychology at the Faculty of Science at the University of Geneva.

Piaget has devoted his exceptional research and theoretical talents to the systematic understanding of the mental evolution of the child, as well as to problems of epistemology. Many of his works have been translated into numerous languages and some of them are now regarded as classics in the field. Piaget has received honorary degrees from universities around the world. He is the founder of the Center for the Study of Genetic Epistemology in Geneva.

DAVID ELKIND is Professor of Psychology and Director of Graduate Training in Developmental Psychology at the University of Rochester. He was Associate Professor and Director of the Child Study Center at the University of Denver. As a National Science Foundation Senior Postdoctoral Fellow, Professor Elkind spent a year (1964-1965) at Piaget's Center for the Study of Genetic Epistemology in Geneva. He has published more than fifty articles in psychology and his work has appeared in such publications as *Child Development*, *Journal of Abnormal Psychology*, *Journal of Educational Psychology*, *Journal of Genetic Psychology*, *Mental Hygiene* and the *Journal for the Scientific Study of Religion*.

ANITA TENZER holds doctoral degrees in philosophy from the Sorbonne in Paris and in clinical psychology from Columbia University. She has worked for many years in publishing in Europe and the U.S. Dr. Tenzer is now a practicing psychologist in New York City.